THE WOMEN'S GUIDE TO RUNNING

WELCOME to Health & Fitness Women's Guide to Running! Maybe you haven't run since school or you've been dabbling for a while and want to step your programme up a gear. Whatever your level, we're here to steer you through every aspect of running. From lacing up your trainers right through to race-day preparation, the following chapters are brimming with tips, techniques and tools to help rev up your running. Think of it as your indispensible and inspirational running coach!

Cover photography Nigel Riches
Photography Nigel Riches
Models Triinu @ Zone Models,
Genevieve @ Nevs, Hollie @ W Athletic
Editors Mary Comber, Antonia Kanczula
Art editors Holly White, Victoria Hill
Design Louise Browne
Sub-editors Jane Walsh, Sharon Gray,
Emma Morris, Margaret Bartlett

Bookazine manager Dharmesh Mistry
Digital production manager Nicky Baker
Production director Robin Ryan
MagBook advertising manager
Katie Wood
Managing director of advertising
Julian Lloyd-Evans
Newstrade director David Barker

Editorial director Pete Muir
Publisher Nicola Bates
Group managing director Ian Westwood
Chief operating officer Brett Reynolds
Group finance director Ian Leggett
Chief executive James Tye
Chairman Felix Dennis

MAG**BOOK**

The 'Magbook' brand is a trademark of Dennis Publishing Ltd, 30 Cleveland St, London W1T 4JD.
Company registered in England. All material © Dennis Publishing Ltd, licensed by Felden 2010,
and may not be reproduced in whole or part without the consent of the publishers.

Women's Guide to Running ISBN 1-78106-000-2

To license this product please contact Ornella Roccoletti on +44 (0) 20 7907 6134 or email
ornella_roccoletti@dennis.co.uk

While every care was taken during the production of this Magbook, the publishers cannot be
held responsible for the accuracy of the information or any consequence arising from it. Dennis
Publishing takes no responsibility for the companies advertising in this Magbook. The paper
used within this Magbook is produced from sustainable fibre, manufactured by mills with a valid
chain of custody. Printed at BGP.

The health and fitness information presented in this book is an educational resource and is not
intended as a substitute for medical advice.

Consult your doctor or healthcare professional before performing any of the exercises
described in this book or any other exercise programme, particularly if you are pregnant, or if
you are elderly or have chronic or recurring medical conditions. Do not attempt any of the
exercises while under the influence of alcohol or drugs.

Discontinue any exercise that causes you pain or severe discomfort and consult a medical expert.
Neither the author of the information nor the producer nor distributors of such information make
any warranty of any kind in regard to the content of the information presented in this book.

CHANGE

YOUR PACE

The Edge is arguably the most comprehensively formulated and advanced energy formula available on the market today.

During strenuous sporting activity, the body is subject to large energy demands, dehydration, muscle damage, free radical damage and reduced immunity.

The Edge® covers every angle with;

- A precise combination of glucose polymers and pure crystalline fructose (HyperCarbs™) which has been scientifically proven to deliver an extra 30% energy in comparison to glucose alone.

- Ultra pure whey protein isolate (ClearPro™) provides a secondary source of energy as well as a source of branch chain amino acids to help prevent muscle breakdown and speed recovery after exercise.

- Mineral and electrolyte complex (PlasmaMax™) which replaces a comprehensive array of vital minerals, trace minerals and electrolytes lost when sweating during strenuous exercise.

An optimal array of antioxidants (Anti Oxidant Collection) scientifically proven to assist the body's antioxidant defence system. As a result, The Edge® could offer increased protection and faster recovery compared to energy drinks without antioxidants.

Probiotics which can boost the immune system and therefore aid recovery.

Some energy drinks address some of these problems but few get close to addressing all of the demands placed on the body in the way that The Edge® does. It really could help you change your pace.

The Edge®

Part of our Energy & Endurance range

Find out more about our products at:

www.reflex-nutrition.com

reflex®
Tomorrow's Nutrition Today™

Get NOTICED!

Dietrim®
CLA (Conjugated Linoleic Acid)
Chromium, Cinnamon Bark
Papaya Extract & Co-Q10

Helps maintain a healthy metabolism
Ideal during any exercise programme
60 soft gel capsules

VITABIOTICS

Contains
Tonalin CLA®
The Shape Of Things To Come™

Dietrim®
CAPSULES

Achieving the sort of figure that gets you noticed can be a real challenge.
Dietrim® provides advanced dietary support for when you are working hard to maintain a fit and healthy looking body.
Each capsule contains 26 ingredients for all round health, including biotin and iodine, which <u>play a role in metabolism and in controlling metabollic rate</u>. It also features Tonalin CLA® (Conjugated Linoleic Acid), a scientifically researched ingredient that is derived from the Safflower plant. Dietrim® helps safeguard your nutritional intake if you are on a dieting programme*, or during exercise, without the need for an additional multivitamin.
<u>So let Dietrim® help maintain a healthy you!</u>

Available from Boots, Superdrug, Holland & Barrett, Lloyds pharmacy, Waitrose, pharmacies and health stores or dietrim.co.uk
For more information contact Vitabiotics on 020 8955 2662 or write to us at 1 Apsley Way, London NW2 7HF
Nutritional supplements may benefit those with nutritionally inadequate diets.*This product has not been proven to aid in weight reduction.

Ω **VITABIOTICS**

Health &Fitness MAGAZINE

CONTENTS

52

28

54

Health &Fitness
MAGAZINE

124

72

98

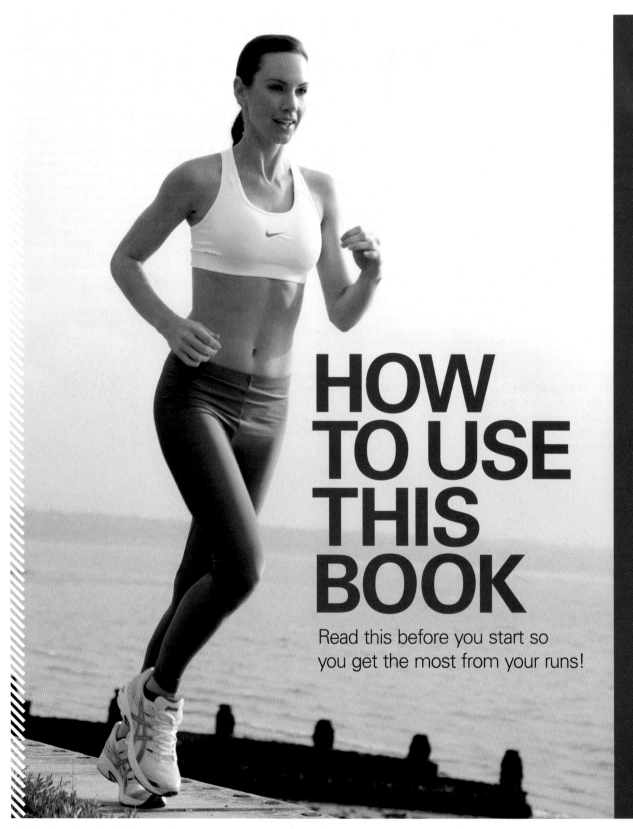

HOW TO USE THIS BOOK

Read this before you start so you get the most from your runs!

There are many reasons to love running, but perhaps the greatest attraction is it's just about as accessible as exercise gets. It's kit-light, there are no rules, few restrictions and it's open to everyone, meaning you don't have to be an elite athlete to reap the benefits – which are numerous.

As with anything in life though, it pays to do some planning before you don your trainers, not only to protect your body from injury but also to guarantee your motivation levels remain high and your relationship with running has staying power.

We've designed this book in a progressive way so we can be with you through the whole journey. So, while it's definitely worth delving into every chapter, look for the section that is specially dedicated to you.

1. A COMPLETE BEGINNER?

A slow and steady approach is vital when you're starting out, and this is the theme at the heart of our 'Getting Started' section (pages 18–43). Flick to these pages if you're new to running or have tried it in the past but couldn't stay committed. It's your indispensable guide to all the basics: buying the right kit, how to stay safe when you're training, the importance of a pre-run warm-up and a post-run stretch. Also in this section is an entry-level walk-run starter plan by personal trainer Cat Dugdale of SUPERchick, which guides you towards running non-stop for 15 to 20 minutes and is guaranteed to get you hooked. Along the way, look out for our specialist Q&As, which will answer any queries you might have.

2. EAGER TO PROGRESS?

So you've mastered running continuously for 20 minutes and you're chomping at the bit? Then our 'Up and Running' section (pages 44–71) is for you. It's all about refining your running and increasing your motivation levels to commit yourself completely to running.

As well as giving you expert tips on technique and improving your form, we'll help you branch out, explore different terrains, plot challenging routes and weatherproof your training so you're running all year round. This is also the perfect time to sample the joys of mass running events, so we've sneaked in two very achievable plans (5k and 10k) to get you started.

3. AN AMBITIOUS RUNNER?

You've well and truly caught the bug and have been running for a few months now. Even if you don't feel like the most competitive runner in the world, we want to show you that feeding your ambition and pushing your body further can offer a multitude of benefits.

The 'Run Ahead' section (pages 72–91) includes chapters on training drills, which we've kept as straightforward as possible; running technology, the gadgets and gizmos that could turbo-charge your regime; cross-training, and we help you – yes, you – complete your first half or full marathon.

4. FOR EVERYONE

Don't forget to look at the two closing sections of the book. You'll find a wealth of nutritional information, advice on strength training and a glossary of UK races, which are suitable for beginners and those with more running experience.

Good luck!

WHY RUN?

Discover the amazing benefits of running and how identifying your goals will help super-charge your training

There isn't a week that goes by without a new snippet of research showing just how great running is for your body and mind. Simple, cheap and versatile it may be, but running is totally empowering and replete with benefits.

IT'S GREAT FOR YOUR HEART
Running has many advantages for your heart health. It lowers body fat, blood pressure and the risk of diabetes, as well as raising good cholesterol levels and building heart muscle. Long-term, running will even increase your blood volume by 10 to 15 per cent, further reducing the demand on your heart.

IT BOOSTS YOUR BONES
Running is a form of weight-bearing exercise, meaning it challenges and strengthens the skeleton. An Australian study published in the journal *Medicine & Science in Sports & Exercise* found running regularly strengthens the leg bones of both older and younger women alike.

IT LOWERS YOUR RISK OF BREAST CANCER
A 10-year study of more than 25,000

women by the University of Tromsø in Norway found those who did a vigorous activity such as running for at least four hours a week were 37 per cent less likely to develop breast cancer than sedentary women.

IT KEEPS YOU YOUNG

Talk about anti-ageing! A 21-year study at Stanford University in the US showed runners suffer fewer disabilities, stay active for longer and halve their risk of an early death.

IT MAKES YOU BRAINIER

Strenuous running enhances blood flow and oxygen levels to your brain, improving memory, mental ability and decision-making processes. Researchers at the University of Illinois, testing a group of 18 to 24-year-olds, found they completed mental tasks faster and more accurately after running on a treadmill.

IT INCREASES YOUR SEX DRIVE

Like all forms of aerobic fitness, running can improve blood flow to your reproductive organs and increase your ability to orgasm. Crucially, it also increases body confidence and, as a result, your libido too. A study carried out at the University of Arkansas found people who worked out regularly felt more sexually attractive than their less-active peers.

IT LIFTS YOUR MOOD

The rhythmic nature of running is a stress-busting distraction. And ever heard of 'runner's high'? Researchers in Germany found running really does trigger a flood of endorphins – your body's natural feel-good chemicals – to the brain.

IT ENSURES A HEALTHIER PREGNANCY AND BIRTH

Women who exercise during pregnancy report higher energy levels and better sleep patterns, and are less likely to suffer with gestational diabetes, varicose veins and pre-eclampsia. They also report sounder sleep patterns, less constipation and indigestion. Research shows women who exercise tend to have higher-birth-weight babies than sedentary women. However, pregnancy is not the time to take up running for the first time.

IT IRONS OUT HORMONAL UPS AND DOWNS

One study, published in the journal *Fertility and Sterility,* found women who ran an average of 12 miles a week for six months reported fewer PMS-related symptoms, such as breast tenderness and bloating. In addition, US studies show exercise may help reduce stress, anxiety, and depression in post-menopausal women.

IT KEEPS YOU TRIM

Lest we forget! As well as boosting muscle tone in the lower body, running burns more calories per minute than almost any other exercise. A person weighing 60kg burns around 300 calories per half hour of steady running. Running a seven-minute mile will burn a whopping 1,000 calories an hour.

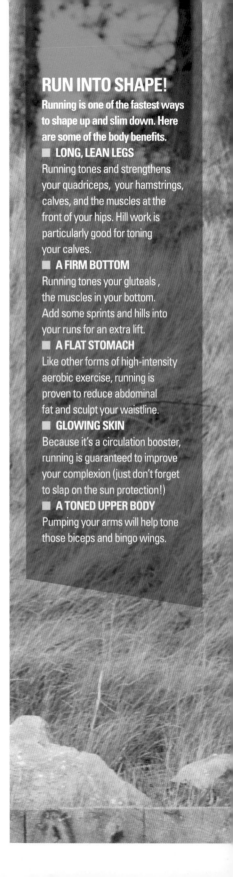

RUN INTO SHAPE!

Running is one of the fastest ways to shape up and slim down. Here are some of the body benefits.

■ **LONG, LEAN LEGS**

Running tones and strengthens your quadriceps, your hamstrings, calves, and the muscles at the front of your hips. Hill work is particularly good for toning your calves.

■ **A FIRM BOTTOM**

Running tones your gluteals, the muscles in your bottom. Add some sprints and hills into your runs for an extra lift.

■ **A FLAT STOMACH**

Like other forms of high-intensity aerobic exercise, running is proven to reduce abdominal fat and sculpt your waistline.

■ **GLOWING SKIN**

Because it's a circulation booster, running is guaranteed to improve your complexion (just don't forget to slap on the sun protection!)

■ **A TONED UPPER BODY**

Pumping your arms will help tone those biceps and bingo wings.

WHAT KIND OF RUNNER ARE YOU?

Identifying your personality type will help you tailor your goals and plan your strategy.

YOU'RE A SOCIALITE

Exercise is part of your social life. You feed off other people's company and veer towards high-octane team sports or activities.
GOALS: Add a social component – finding a running buddy or joining a club may elevate your fitness, especially if you're with runners who are particularly focused or serious. Try setting yourself goals or following a training plan to give structure to your running.

YOU'RE AN IMPROVER

You use exercise to aid your life. You're not alone – a study by the Temple University in Philadelphia found women are more likely to run to lose weight or improve their mood.
GOALS: Don't set yourself unattainably large goals – or you'll feel like running is something you 'have' to do, rather than 'want' to do. Concentrate on steadily building up distances and tweaking your technique so you learn to love running. Remember to reward yourself!

YOU'RE AN ACHIEVER

You're results-driven and extra-competitive. You grab everything in life with both hands and like to have structured, lofty aims.
GOALS: Be careful of pushing your body too far, too soon – read our injury prevention plan on page 64. Factor other kinds of exercise into your weekly programme so you don't burn out. You'll thrive on races, but start with 5k or 10k events rather than going straight for a half or full marathon.

YOU'RE A BALANCER

You exercise out of a pure love of it; you enjoy the freedom it gives you and cherish the feeling of pushing yourself.
GOALS: Shake up your programme now and then, stepping it up a gear so your enjoyment is constantly fired. You'll enjoy the thrill of trail or off-road running, so check out our terrain feature (page 56) and the events section (page 124) for the UK's most scenic races.

BE INSPIRED!

Meet three women whose fitness – and lives – have been transformed by running

'COMPLETING MY FIRST RACE FELT LIKE WINNING OLYMPIC GOLD!'

Maija Bissett, 33, from St Neots, Cambridgeshire rediscovered the joys of running in her 30s and says it's helped transform her body and her wellbeing.

'Growing up in Finland, I was into running big time, particularly sprinting, and competed at quite a high level but working life got in the way of exercise in my 20s.

'After I gave birth to my daughter Grace in 2002, I was so consumed with motherhood I didn't think about exercise and relied on ready meals. Steadily the pounds crept on. In 2006, my brother died unexpectedly while I was pregnant with my son. I was very unhappy and constantly tired. At my heaviest, I was a size 20–22 and had little confidence.

'In 2007, aged 30, a friend asked me to sponsor her for a Race For Life. I thought, "if she can do it, why can't I?" and entered the Great North Run half marathon. I started running gradually. At first I could only manage about five- to 10-minute portions, but days turned into months and I fell back in love with running. I became more conscious of what I ate and come race day I'd got down to a size 18! It was emotional and hard, but my husband, kids and in-laws and buzz of the whole day carried me through. I raised £1,340 for a heart charity in the memory of my brother and finished in three hours 27 minutes!

'Since then, running has been a constant in my life and now I'm a re-energised size 12/14. In 2010, I decided to run 250km in a year over several races for the Alzheimer's Society,

'I'LL NEVER WIN PRIZES BUT COMPETING IS A REAL THRILL'

a cause dear to me as my aunt and godfather have the disease.

'I'll never win prizes, but competing against myself is a real thrill.'

* *The Alzheimer's Society is Bupa's chosen charity for the 2011 Bupa Great Run Series. Visit www. alzheimers.org.uk/greatrun*

'I BELIEVE ANYONE AND EVERYONE CAN RUN!'

Kathryn Betts, 27, from London, was inspired by work colleagues to start running and hasn't looked back since.

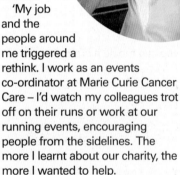

'Before I discovered running I didn't exercise. I wasn't lazy, it just felt like I didn't need it.

'My job and the people around me triggered a rethink. I work as an events co-ordinator at Marie Curie Cancer Care – I'd watch my colleagues trot off on their runs or work at our running events, encouraging people from the sidelines. The more I learnt about our charity, the more I wanted to help.

'Five years ago, I signed up for my first 10k with a friend, Claire. I gave myself six months to train for it and started off steadily – run, walk, run, walk around a block near home, as many times as I could manage, three times a week. Gradually, I branched out, challenged myself with longer runs and discovered I was quite competitive.

'The benefits were apparent almost immediately – I remember my first breakthrough, two weeks in, when I thought "I'm not out of breath, hooray!" It was a true milestone. It got easier and easier and I felt more energised. After a few months, I'd definitely toned up and felt more body confident.

'That first race was nerve-wracking but totally uplifting. One of the things that really struck me was the range of people taking part – it wasn't full of sleek athletes but people like me. And it felt amazing to cross the finish line. That buzz has got me hooked!

'What I love so much about running is the fact you can do it anywhere, it isn't expensive and

'I REMEMBER WHEN I THOUGHT, I'M NOT OUT OF BREATH, HOORAY'

you can mould it around your life.

'I've done races every year since my first 10k – including a very gruelling marathon in Melbourne, Australia last year during a six-month career break. I never would have expected to progress to a full marathon from those small, tentative first runs I did around the block!

'I've started doing a lot more cycling, so I'm pondering a duathlon at the moment and I really want to do the Virgin London Marathon. My mum passed away from cancer recently and this has made me even more determined to raise money through running.

'I don't think I have a natural running ability, but I'm tough and I love the feeling it gives me. I'm proof that anyone can give it a go!'
* *Marie Curie Cancer Care offers an events programme to suit everyone. Visit www.mariecurie.org.uk/ challenge and help provide more nursing care for terminally ill people.*

'WHEN YOU'RE RUNNING, YOU'RE IN YOUR OWN BUBBLE.'

Inspired by Eddie Izzard but with no prior race experience, 22-year-old Maggi Broadbent, from Somerset, ran 14 marathons in 14 days.

'In spring 2010, I was watching Eddie Izzard's 43-marathon Sport Relief challenge and felt totally inspired. My friend Rosie has diabetes and we'd discussed fundraising for Diabetes UK so Eddie's odyssey struck a chord. I decided to do 14 marathons – I thought a week would go too quickly – and designed a plan with friends who've done marathons before. I knew it would be difficult and painful at times, but I was sure I was strong-willed enough to see it through.

'Although I've always loved running, I wasn't particularly experienced and I'd never done a competitive event before so I built my miles up gradually. I also started eating more healthily and cut down on alcohol. I plotted my routes and drove them to check how feasible they were. It was all very ad hoc – but I did get some expert input! I wrote to Professor John Brewer, a sports scientist quoted in a few articles about Eddie. His top tip was to aim to do each marathon in six hours, to give me recovery time for the next.

'When donations started coming in, I knew I couldn't back out. Finishing the first of my 14 marathons in five-and-a-half hours gave me a huge boost. I battled through sweltering hot weather, torrential rain, horrible hills, and some nasty blisters. I even got

lost a few times but my fortnight on the road was full of highpoints. It was fantastic to be outdoors in such beautiful countryside and I had tons of support. My mum would drive me to the start line each day and meet me at intervals with food and drinks. On my third day, a friend from uni came along as my marathon buddy and on the ninth day, runners from a local club joined me.

'My final marathon on August 26 took around six hours and, full of adrenaline, I was welcomed home to our local pub by a band of supporters. I stayed on a high for a few days. Originally, I'd aimed to raise £1,000, but lots of people heard me on regional news or met me along the way, so I far exceeded this. It was a huge personal achievement and

'IT WAS FANTASTIC TO BE OUTDOORS AND I HAD TONS OF SUPPORT'

hopefully I've helped to raise awareness of diabetes too.

'It's still a real confidence boost to think back on what I did. I'm definitely going to plan a new challenge soon, but I'm not sure what it will be, and until then I'll carry on running. It's my time – I can get totally lost in it and it's a great outlet. If you're thinking about running but wavering, my advice is avoid putting up any mental barriers. You can definitely give it a go, we're all much tougher and more capable than we think we are.'
* *www.diabetes.org.uk*

PHOTOGRAPHY: David Ryle

GETTING STARTED

One of the biggest mistakes you can make when starting out is to set the bar too high. While optimism is definitely a good thing, expecting too much of yourself may leave you feeling deflated – not to mention sore!

Like most things in life, in order to fall in love with running, you need to nurture your relationship. Avoid the all-or-nothing approach and, above all else, pace yourself.

This section of the book will help you slowly build up some sound physical foundations and self-confidence. By the end, we guarantee you'll feel empowered!

SHOES: ASICS
www.asics.co.uk

IF YOU'RE NEW TO
EXERCISE, CHECK
YOUR HEALTH

RUNNERS'
MOT

Make sure you're
fit for exercise…

So far, we've emphasised the ease and convenience of running, but this assumes that you're fit and ready to give it a go. If you're totally new to exercise, recovering from illness or injury, or you're concerned about an existing health problem, you may want a check-up before you start running. If you answer yes to any of the following questions, see your GP to discuss your suitability for running.

1 **Have you been inactive for a year or more?**
☐ YES ☐ NO

2 **Have you ever been diagnosed with a heart condition or high blood pressure?**
☐ YES ☐ NO

3 **Do you smoke or are you a former smoker?**
☐ YES ☐ NO

4 **Do you have asthma or have you ever suffered from asthma?**
☐ YES ☐ NO

5 **Is there a history of premature heart problems in your close family (parent or sibling – under 55 in men, under 65 in women)?**
☐ YES ☐ NO

6 **Do you ever experience chest pain or dizziness during exercise?**
☐ YES ☐ NO

7 **Have you been diagnosed with a chronic bone or joint problem such as arthritis or osteoporosis?**
☐ YES ☐ NO

8 **Are you diabetic?**
☐ YES ☐ NO

9 **Are you trying for a baby, pregnant or have you recently given birth?**
☐ YES ☐ NO

10 **Do you have a BMI (body mass index) of more than 26?**
☐ YES ☐ NO

11 **Have you been diagnosed with a chronic condition that may cause problems?**
☐ YES ☐ NO

Q&A
SHOULD RUNNING HURT?

If you're new to the sport, expect to feel a bit achy a day or two after your run. DOMS (delayed onset muscle soreness) is the name physiologists give to this discomfort, which is the result of microscopic tears in the muscle fibres and the release of lactic acid into the tissues.

Provided you warm up and stretch adequately, and cool down and stretch, then rest and take things easy if necessary afterwards, this shouldn't be a huge problem and your body will gradually adapt as you continue to run. If the soreness lingers, it could be a sign you've been pushing yourself too hard. If you feel any sharp pain, or pain that gets worse when you run, rest or see a sports physiotherapist for advice.

Thanks to Nick Englefield, fitness supervisor, Crystal Palace National Sports Centre, for additional research.

TEST YOUR
LEVEL

Use these DIY tests to measure your fitness and monitor your running progress as you train

So you're kitted up and you've passed our health MOT? Establishing your basic level of fitness is the next step. This will help you determine how far and how often to run and help you identify some short-term goals.

We've designed a set of very straightforward home tests you can use to assess some of the physical qualities you need for running. Repeat them every six to 12 weeks and record the results so you can keep a motivating record of your improvement.

For the results to be accurate, do the tests in the same circumstances each time – in the same order, in the same environment, with the same equipment after doing the same warm-up. Above all else, be honest with yourself about your initial level of fitness so you can ensure your programme is right for you.

CLOTHING: American Apparel, www.americanapparel.co.uk; Casall, www.casallstore.com; Sweaty Betty, www.sweatybetty.com; Nike, www.nikestore.com

AEROBIC FITNESS
THE STEP-UP TEST
Use a bench or step as close to 12 inches (30.5cm) in height as possible. Stand facing the step. When you're ready to begin, start the clock or stopwatch and follow an 'up, up, down, down' action. You should be doing 24 of these complete steps in one minute – a steady pace. When three minutes are up, stop and count your pulse (use your wrist or neck) for one full minute.

What the results mean

AGE	18–25	26–35	36–45	46–55
EXCELLENT	<85 BPM (BEATS PER MIN)	<85	<89	<95
GOOD	85–93	85–92	89–96	95–101
ABOVE AVERAGE	96–102	95–101	100–104	104–110
AVERAGE	104–110	104–110	107–112	113–118
BELOW AVERAGE	113–120	113–119	115–120	120–124
POOR	122–131	122–129	124–132	126–132
VERY POOR	135–169	134–171	137–169	137–171

(i) As you get fitter, you'll return to your resting heart rate more quickly. An average resting rate is 70 beats per minute, but it varies hugely. Use a heart rate monitor to test it or check your pulse on your wrist when you've been sitting down for a few minutes.

SPEED
A TIMED ONE-MILE RUN OR WALK
Plot a flat, one-mile route or use a treadmill set at a one per cent gradient. Put in maximum effort and walk the mile (1,600 metres or 1.6km), aiming for less than 15 minutes.

What the results mean

Under 6 minutes > **EXCELLENT**
Under 8 minutes > **VERY GOOD**
Under 10 minutes > **GOOD**
10–12 minutes > **SATISFACTORY**

(i) If you took longer than 12 minutes you should begin your running programme with brisk walking, not with running. Walk three to four times a week for about 30 to 45 minutes, gently increasing speed over a few weeks. It takes about six weeks for your muscles to adjust, so be patient!

CORE STRENGTH
THE PLANK TEST
A strong core powers your body in exercise and everyday life and can help protect against injury, especially in your lower back. There's no stipulated way to measure your core strength but timing how long you can hold plank position is probably the best gauge. Lie face-down on the floor, then push yourself up onto your forearms and toes and clasp your hands. Keep your gaze down and your body in a straight line from your ears to your toes. Ask a friend to time you and make sure you keep good form throughout.

What the results mean
If you can hold the plank for 45 to 60 seconds, you have good core strength. Try to improve by a few seconds each time you do it.

(i) To boost your core strength, make sure you engage your core each time you run, by imagining that your belly button is moving towards your spine. You can do this move at any point during your daily life too. Flick to page 80 to find out how yoga and Pilates could help you.

FLEXIBILITY
THE SIT AND REACH TEST
You'll need a long ruler or tape measure and some floor space for this one. Sit on the floor with your legs straight out in front of you. Exhale and reach forward as far as you can in a smooth motion, and hold this position for two seconds. Record the distance between your toes and the tips of your fingers, either before your toes or past them.

What the results mean

Over 21cm past toes > **EXCELLENT**
11–20cm past toes > **GOOD**
0–10cm past toes > **AVERAGE**
10cm before toes to level with toes > **BELOW AVERAGE**
Under 10cm away from toes > **POOR**

(i) To prevent injury and improve your stride, make sure you warm up before and stretch after your runs. If your flexibility is particularly poor, you might also benefit from yoga and Pilates.

COOL KIT

These essentials will help you look – and, crucially, feel – like a serious runner

Brooks Ravenna 2 trainers
www.brooksrunning.co.uk

There are exciting new innovations in running kit every season it seems, and it's easy to be seduced by hot trends. But the only essentials you really need to buy are good trainers, a sports bra and socks made specifically for running; everything else is down to personal taste and your budget.

1 SHOES

Your shoes should always be your first consideration. Don't second-guess your gait; go to a specialist running store, particularly if you've never been fitted before. If you're a keen runner or in training for an event that requires daily runs, it may be worth your while buying two pairs so you can alternate them, to give the padding time to recover.

The 'barefoot' running movement has been gathering pace recently, but you should only try it if you're an experienced runner and have access to safe routes.

Reebok Premier ZigTech Short 3.5"
www.reebok.com

2 RUN-SPECIFIC LEGGINGS, SHORTS OR CAPRI PANTS

Fitted bottoms are designed to prevent water-logging, chafing and tripping, and will make running much more comfortable. Most have hidden pockets (normally just below the small of your back) and they may also have reflective panels. Go for thicker, matt fabrics for winter runs.

Do Running Women's Sheer Performance Capri Half Tight
www.prodirectrunning.com

**Do Running Women's
Crossover Running Jacket**
www.prodirectrunning.com

**Run Breeze
Anti-blister Sock**
www.runbreeze.com

Moving Comfort Juno Bra
www.movingcomfort.com

4 WICKING TOP

We don't want to be dictatorial; when it comes to running, you can wear what you want – to a certain extent. However, wicking, breathable fabrics are among the greatest innovations for runners and are an essential investment. Unlike cotton, they don't get heavy when you sweat and dry super-fast, so they keep you looking and smelling fresh. Added extras, such as fabrics with antibacterial or SPF sun-protective properties, are also worth considering.

5 WINDPROOF JACKET

A lightweight jacket will provide an extra layer you can whip off at a moment's notice (a great idea in winter). Choose one with secret pockets, so you can carry essentials such as your keys or phone. It's also a good idea to go for one with high-visibility reflective panels, for running in the dark. However, be aware there's a difference between 'showerproof', which will only provide a barrier against light rain, and completely 'waterproof'.

6 BRA

Everyone's breasts jiggle when they run, even small ones: a 2009 study on breast movement at Portsmouth University revealed some breasts move up to eight inches during a run, which is not only uncomfortable but can cause sagging in the connective tissue of the breast, otherwise known as Cooper's ligaments. For support, comfort and confidence, a well-fitting sports bra is a must. It might be an idea to get professionally fitted, but in general, look for a fit that's snug but not so tight it restricts your breathing. The straps shouldn't dig into your shoulders and look for seamless or flat-seam designs to prevent chafing. How long your bra lasts depends on how often you use it, but the general recommendation is that you replace it every six months.

3 SOCKS

We know what you're thinking. Socks aren't the sexiest part of your kit, but they perform a vital role, providing cushioned support exactly where you need it and wicking (carrying and locking away) sweat to prevent blisters. Look for high-tech fabrics, such as COOLMAX, and go for double-layered designs to prevent friction. Once you've found your perfect match, buy a few pairs because they wear out faster than you think!

OPTIONAL EXTRAS

1 BACK OR BUM-BELT PACK

Essential if you're a long-distance runner or you run to work, this has enough room to transport everything you need, but won't move around or chafe your skin. For shorter runs, choose run-specific upper-arm or wrist storage options. For long runs on warm days, you could use a hydration pack backpack with a water bladder inside and a flexible drinking tube.

2 RUNNING WATCH

Reach your fitness goals with a watch by keeping track of your daily exercise, measuring your distance traveled, calories burned and average pace.

3 SUN VISOR OR LIGHTWEIGHT CAP

A visor or cap will keep glaring light out of your face and protect it from damaging UV rays.

4 WATER BOTTLE

Look for a water bottle with a hole in the middle so you can easily hold it as you run.

5 THERMALS

If you're particularly prone to the cold, it's worth investing in a thermal sport-specific base layer.

6 SUNGLASSES

Ultra-light, wrap-around runner's shades are important for safety – not just as a style statement. UV light can damage your retinas and, in the long term, can even contribute to AMD (age-related macular degeneration). Sports glasses normally have 100 per cent UVA and UVB protection.

7 GLOVES

Protecting your extremities will make winter runs much more bearable. Choose thermal sports-specific fabrics and make sure they'll fit in a pocket once you warm up.

8 COMPRESSION CLOTHING

These tight-fitting garments are thought to prevent fatigue by curbing muscle vibration and are much loved by elite athletes.

2 **Soleus 10k Regular Watch**
www.soleusrunning.com

1 **Salomon XA 20 Women's Backpack**
www.salomonrunning.com

4 **Sweatshop 500ml drinks bottle**
www.sweatshop.co.uk

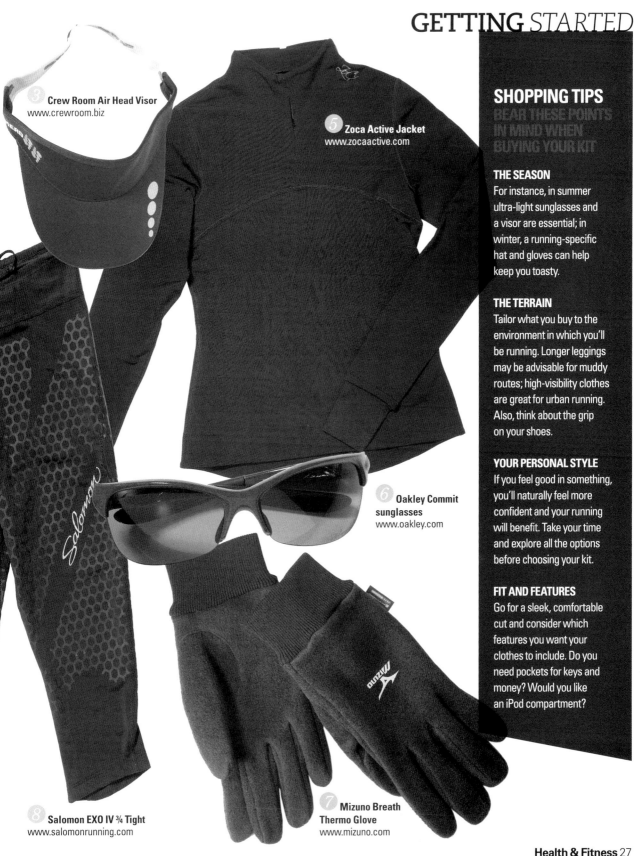

3 **Crew Room Air Head Visor**
www.crewroom.biz

5 **Zoca Active Jacket**
www.zocaactive.com

6 **Oakley Commit sunglasses**
www.oakley.com

8 **Salomon EXO IV ¾ Tight**
www.salomonrunning.com

7 **Mizuno Breath Thermo Glove**
www.mizuno.com

SHOPPING TIPS
BEAR THESE POINTS IN MIND WHEN BUYING YOUR KIT

THE SEASON
For instance, in summer ultra-light sunglasses and a visor are essential; in winter, a running-specific hat and gloves can help keep you toasty.

THE TERRAIN
Tailor what you buy to the environment in which you'll be running. Longer leggings may be advisable for muddy routes; high-visibility clothes are great for urban running. Also, think about the grip on your shoes.

YOUR PERSONAL STYLE
If you feel good in something, you'll naturally feel more confident and your running will benefit. Take your time and explore all the options before choosing your kit.

FIT AND FEATURES
Go for a sleek, comfortable cut and consider which features you want your clothes to include. Do you need pockets for keys and money? Would you like an iPod compartment?

SHOE GUIDE

Your running shoes are the most important – and expensive – part of your kit, so you need to give them careful consideration before you buy

SHOES: Brooks
www.brooksrunning.co.uk

to fit your ankle bone neatly – it shouldn't chafe or dig in too deeply.

6. HEEL CUP A slightly rigid, cupped-shaped piece of plastic on the inside of the trainer to hold your heel in place and control the motion of your rear foot.

1. TOE BOX This should be roomy but also provide protection for your toes. Look for shoes suited to the shape and angle of your toes – and go for a reinforced toe box if you're planning to go off road.

2. LUGS These enhance the grip of the shoe on the ground.

3. UPPER The part of the shoe made of fabric, above the sole.

4. INSOLE The removable and supportive sole inside your shoe.

5. HEEL TAB This is contoured

7. MIDSOLE Some say this is the most important component of trainers, as it provides cushioning and stability.

8. OUTSOLE The underneath of the shoe, usually crafted from carbon rubber or a similar material. It needs to be firm enough to offer plenty of traction, yet flexible enough to bend.

9. LACES Some trainers come with toggle laces, but most are traditional lace-ups.

RunBreeze

FOCUS ON YOUR GOALS. NOT YOUR FEET.

THE ANTI-BLISTER SOCK £8

Featuring double-layered technology, the two layers rub against each other instead of your foot. This helps to prevent blisters, which means you can run easier, freer, faster.

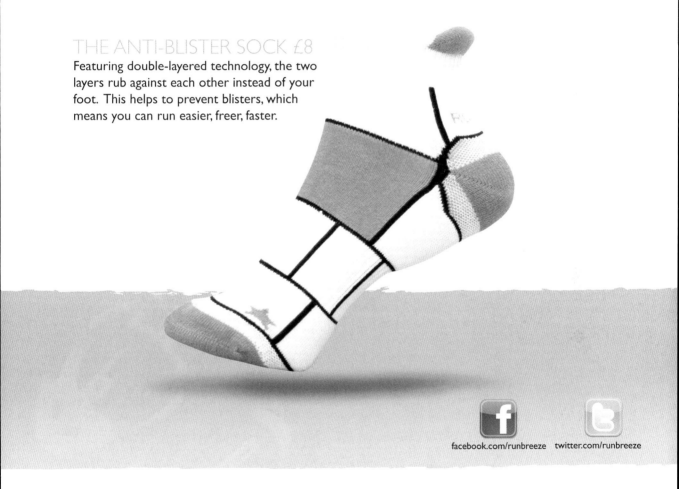

facebook.com/runbreeze   twitter.com/runbreeze

SAVE 10%* when you purchase any RunBreeze technical sock online today. Visit www.runbreeze.com and enter code womensrunning10 to claim your discount. Plus, free P&P on all orders over £10.

THE SHOE FOR YOU

Your trainers should be tailored to the type of foot strike you have – in other words, how your feet land when you run – plus where you intend to run, whether on road, track or trail

WHAT'S YOUR GAIT?

The way you run (your biomechanics) will affect the type of shoes you wear. A 'normal' foot lands on the outside of the heel and then, to absorb shock, rolls (or pronates) slightly inwards. If your foot pronates too much, you'll need a motion-control shoe to prevent long-term overuse injuries. Similarly, if your foot doesn't roll enough ('supination'), often as a result of inflexibility or high arches, you'll also need shoes with corrective features.

You should visit a specialist running store to get your gait assessed, but you can look at the footprint you leave on a tiled floor when your foot's damp or check the soles of your shoes to see where the tread is worn to get an idea.

NORMAL PRONATION
Your wet footprint should have a connection between your forefoot and heel and show a moderately sized arch.
Recommended trainers
You can wear neutral shoes with basic control features.

TOO MUCH PRONATION
If your footprint shows the entire base of your foot, you are likely to have flat feet and over-pronate.
Recommended trainers
Opt for motion-control and stability shoes.

NOT ENOUGH PRONATION
A high-arched foot will leave a print showing only your heel and toes.
Recommended trainers
Your trainers should absorb shock: look for well-cushioned neutral designs.

New Balance 1080 trainers
www.shopnewbalance.co.uk

1. ROAD OR PARK
Your shoes will have shallow tread and lots of cushioning to absorb the shock of running on hard surfaces.

Newton Distance shoe
www.newtonrunning.co.uk

Brooks Adrenaline GTS
www.brooksrunning.co.uk

adidas ClimaCool Ride trainers
www.adidas.com

2. RACETRACK
You're unlikely to be on the track if you're new to running, but if it's something you decide to explore later on, you'll need lightweight, low-heel racer shoes for speed!

K Swiss Blade-Max Trail shoes
www.kswiss.co.uk

3. TRAIL OR OFF-ROAD

These shoes have grippy outsoles, tough (sometimes waterproof) uppers, good lateral support and moderate cushioning.

Puma FAAS 300 Lightweight Running Shoes
www.puma.com

On Running Cloud Surfer trainers
www.on-running.co.uk

4. GOING 'BAREFOOT'

Wearing trainers that provide a cushionless protective barrier from the ground can help you run more instinctively and realign your technique, but they're best avoided if you're new to running, you run on unpredictable terrain or have an unusual foot strike.

Merrell Barefoot Pace Glove trainers
www.merrell.com

SHOPPING TIPS

By now, you should realise the importance of going to a specialist running store – at the very least, to help you make sense of the confusing language! Expect to pay anything upwards of £60 for a good pair of shoes.

■ To analyse your gait, you'll be expected to run, so wear something appropriate. Some stores will do this with video analysis and ask you to go on a treadmill; others may simply do it by eye and might get you to run outside the shop.

■ Go shopping in the afternoon or early evening. Your feet swell when you run, so leaving the trying-on process until later in the day will help replicate this as your feet also swell a little during the day.

■ Buy your shoes for comfort, rather than style. Your trainers must be comfortable and fit from the outset – don't think you can break them in. If they're too tight, it may lead to black toenails and hard skin. If they're too loose, your feet will slip and slide inside the shoes, causing blisters. They should fit snugly at the heel, with around a thumb's width between your big toe and the end of the shoe. Some brands offer shoes specifically for women, which are narrower at the heel and broader in the forefoot.

WHERE TO BUY

Runner's Need is a London-based chain of specialist stores. Find your nearest at *www.runnersneed.co.uk*
Run and Become has stores in London, Cardiff and Edinburgh. Visit *www.runandbecome.com*
Up and Running has stores throughout the UK and a great online store too. Take a look at *www.upandrunning.co.uk*
Sweatshop also has a thriving network of stores, and an easy-to-navigate web shop too. Visit *www.sweatshop.co.uk*

STAYING SAFE

Don't let your fears get the better of you. Here's how to ward off danger

Provided you follow some common-sense advice, there's no reason to feel scared of getting out and running, wherever and whenever you want. To ramp up your street savviness, you could take a self-defence course.

STRANGER DANGER

Most unwanted attention – of the male jeering kind – is harmless enough and easy to brush-off. For everything else, trust your instincts. If at any point you feel threatened, run to a busy area or shop, where there are plenty of other people. Make sure you always face the oncoming traffic to deter curb-crawlers and if someone stops to ask you something, keep a safe distance and keep moving. On country roads where there are no pavements, keep as far away from passing traffic as possible and be extra-wary on the bends.

We know music is incredibly motivating, but wearing headphones and having the volume ramped up to the max robs you of a valuable commodity when it comes to safety – your hearing. If you're running in fading light or near traffic, it might be a good idea to leave your iPod at home or listen in one ear only.

Always take your phone but avoid chatting on it while you're running – you could get distracted from what's going on around you.

THERE'S SAFETY IN NUMBERS – TRY TO RUN WITH OTHERS

NOCTURNAL RISKS

While we'd recommend you run in daylight, sometimes it's not possible.

Always pre-plan your run and if possible, tell someone at home where you're going and when you plan to get back. Stick to well-lit routes, where there are plenty of people and there's lots of activity around you, and avoid alleyways, quiet wooded areas and shortcuts. Make sure you wear some fluoro or high-vis clothing so cars can see you when you're on the road.

DON'T BE A VICTIM

The rules of street safety apply to running, too. Don't have tempting personal property on show that might arouse the attention of a would-be thief. Keep all your valuable essentials, such as your phone and keys, close to your body.

Shake up your running routine regularly – if you follow the same route at the same time on the same day every week, you may be a vulnerable target. For extra safety-proofing, invest in a wrist personal alarm (try the Silva 56015 with pedometer; £19.99 from www.heartratemonitor.co.uk); hopefully you won't have to use the alarm, but it may increase your street confidence and you can use the pedometer to motivate you to run further. Finally, there's safety in numbers – try to run with other people, such as club members or friends. It could elevate your performance too!

Q&A

I'M SCARED OF DOGS – HOW SHOULD I ACT IF ONE APPROACHES ME IN THE PARK?

Bear in mind most dogs just get a little excited and are only trying to be friendly, but in any situation it's always best to act confidently if you see Rover bounding in your direction. Slow down and don't make eye contact, otherwise it could see you as a threat. If you can, head in another direction so the dog doesn't assume you're trying to invade his or her territory and don't look back! If you can't avoid its advances, stay calm and don't make any sudden movements. Say something firm, such as 'no' or 'sit' and if it tries to jump on you, turn to the side.

DYNAMIC WARM-UP

Get your body ready to run with these easy moves

efore any running session, you need to devote some quality time to preparing your body. You might be tempted to do a few static or still stretches, but the secret to good pre-exercise is dynamic movement that mimics the motion of running. Not only will this increase your heart rate, mobilise your joints and get you in the mood for exercise, it will also raise your body temperature and improve your flexibility. In the long term, warming-up is key to your injury prevention plan.

YOUR PRE-RUN ROUTINE

All the following moves have been designed to activate the muscles you'll be using during your runs. Start with some brisk walking and then add in the dynamic exercises, gradually building intensity. Devote around five to 10 minutes to your preparation.

TIP

Keep your back straight as you lunge. If needed, support yourself with your hand on your front thigh (not your knee).

1

HIGH KNEES

Gets the heart rate up, activates your hip flexors and calves, and warms up the upper body.

› Lift your knees as high as possible and pump your arms for 20 reps.

2

BUTT KICKS

Loosens the quadricep muscles at the front of your thighs and prepares the hamstrings (at the back of your thighs) for the landing motion.

› Jog slowly, kicking back with your trailing leg, stretching the quadriceps and kicking your gluteals (your bum muscles) for 20 reps.

3

SMALL WALKING LUNGES

Warms up the hip flexors, switches on the gluteals and raises the heart rate.

› From standing, take a large step forward with your right leg and bend both knees so your front knee is in line with your ankle and your back knee is close to the floor, with your back heel lifted. Continue alternating legs for 20 reps (10 each leg).

TIP
Pull your tummy muscles in throughout this move to work your core and help you maintain your balance.

4

CALF STEP-BACKS

A whole-body exercise that switches on your core and stretches the calves and hip flexors.

> Starting with your feet together, step your right leg behind the body and allow both knees to bend slightly, raising your arms above your head. Return to standing and repeat on the other leg. Perform 20 reps (10 on each leg).

5

TOE TOUCHES

Great for warming up your gluteals, lower back and abdominals.

> Standing on your left leg, bring your right knee up towards your chest and your right foot in front of your left thigh. Bring your left hand in to touch your right foot. Slowly lower your right leg to the floor then repeat on the other side. Perform 20 times (10 on each leg).

6

HIP ROLL

Activates your pelvic area and engages your lower body.

> Stand with your feet hip-distance apart, hands on your hips and knees slightly bent. Make a large clockwise circle with your hips, doing it 10 times. Repeat in opposite direction, also 10 times. You may want to add some gentle neck and shoulder rolls at the end.

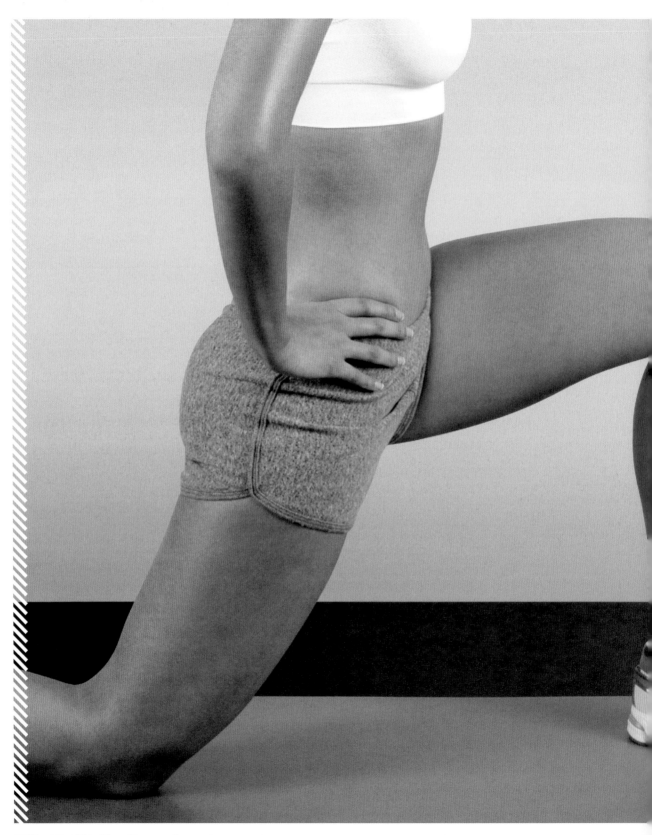

AND STRETCH

Ease your post-run muscles with these tried and tested moves

hen you get to the end of your run, avoid stopping suddenly. Just as you need to gradually build up the intensity of your movements at the start, you need to wind them down afterwards.
A thorough and consistent stretching routine has many benefits. As you run, your muscles contract, so the stretching process is a chance to elongate them. It will also help reduce muscle soreness by speeding up the removal of lactic acid and, in the long-term, protect your body against the rigours of running.

THE GOLDEN RULES OF STRETCHING

■ Don't bounce. Hold each stretch steady, on each side of your body, for 20 to 30 seconds.
■ Only stretch to the point that's comfortable for you – you shouldn't feel discomfort or pain.
■ Make it specific and balanced. Our running stretches focus on the main muscles used in running.
■ Don't stretch beyond the point where you begin to feel tightness in the muscle. Never push through muscle resistance, or stretch to the point of discomfort or pain.
■ You should perform stretches when your body is warm so, although it's advisable to do them straight after a run, you do have a small window of opportunity and you could even do them after a warm post-run bath.

1
KNEELING STRETCH

Stretches your hip flexors and core. If hip flexors are tight they will pull you off balance and your pelvis out of line.

> Kneel on a padded mat or soft flooring. Lunge forward with your left knee, keeping it in line with the ankle. Place your hands on your hips and push hips forward until you feel the stretch. Repeat on other leg.

2
CALF STRETCH

This stretch keeps the calves loose and relieves stress in your Achilles, the tendon that connects the calf muscles to the heel bone.

> Stand in a wide stance with one leg in front of the other and both feet flat on the floor. Lean forward with your front knee bent, keeping your back leg straight. Repeat on the other side.

3
IT BAND STRETCH

Foam rollers are a useful investment for runners, but you could also use a tennis ball for this stretch. Your IT (iliotibial) band runs along the outside of the thigh.

> Lie sideways on a foam roller using arms to support you. Starting at the hip, roll along the IT band for the full length of your thigh, keeping most of your weight on the roller. Repeat on the other side.

TIP
If you feel unsteady balancing on one leg, place your inactive arm on a wall, tree or park bench.

4

BUTTERFLY STRETCH

Loosens up your inner thighs.

> Sit on the floor with the soles of your shoes together. Grasp your ankles and gently push your knees down as far as is comfortable towards the floor. Hold the stretch, don't bounce.

5

HAMSTRING STRETCH

Use any steady surface, such as a stair or park bench, to do this move.

> Extend one leg and place it on a support between shin and thigh height with your foot flexed. Gently bend the supporting leg and tip forward from the hips – don't round your back. Keep the pelvis level until you feel a stretch along the back of your thigh.

6

QUADRICEPS STRETCH

Elongates the muscles at the front of your thighs.

> Standing tall, lift your right foot to your bottom and grasp your ankle with your right hand. Pull in your abdominal muscles and gently pull your foot up with your hand, keeping your knees together and ensuring you don't arch your back.

STARTER PLAN

Personal trainer **Cat Dugdale** guides you from brisk walking to a continuous run of 15 to 20 minutes

QUICK TIPS

• *Remember to warm up and stretch after each session, using our guides on pages 34–41.*

• *At least twice a week, find the time to do our strength-building exercises on pages 112–123. You can tag them on to the end of one of your walk/run sessions. Test your fitness at the beginning and the end of the programme.*

• *When you start running, make sure you're running tall and smoothly – see page 48 for our technique guide.*

WEEK	MONDAY	TUESDAY	WEDNESDAY	THURSDAY	FRIDAY	SATURDAY	SUNDAY
1	30 min power walk	REST	Cross-train	30 min power walk	REST	Run 1 min walk 2 min x 6	REST
2	30 min power walk	REST	Cross-train	30 min power walk	REST	Run 1 min walk 2 min x 6	REST
3	Run 2 min walk 2 min x 6	REST	Cross-train	30 min power walk	REST and reward yourself with a massage	Run 2 min walk 2 min x 6	REST
4	Run 5 min walk 2 min x 4	REST	Cross-train	30 min power walk	REST	Run 5 min walk 2 min x 4	REST
5	Run 10 min walk 5 min run 5 min	REST	Cross-train	30 min power walk	REST and reward yourself with a massage	Run 5 min walk 1 min x 4	REST
6	Run 15 min walk 5 min run 5 min	REST	Cross-train	30 min power walk	REST	Run 20 minutes	REST

STARTER *PLAN*

UP &
RUNNING

So you've caught the bug! This section is all about super-charging your programme so you can foster a life-long commitment to running. From the subtlest of technique tweaks to plotting new routes and exploring new terrains, we show you how to expand your running horizons. But throughout, our message stays the same: be progressive, gradual and consistent with your running and you'll not only stay injury-free but build your confidence enough to complete your first 5k or 10k with a smile on your face!

**HAVE A LONG-TERM
GOAL AS WELL AS SMALL
MANAGEABLE GOALS**

HOW TO PROGRESS

Push things forward with these tips for advancing your running

here's a saying, 'He who moves not forward, goes backward'. Although this philosophical idea wasn't being applied to exercise at the time, its meaning definitely holds true for running.

Whether you're highly ambitious or simply in it for fun, you need to make progress. If you stay at the same level, you're less likely to reach your potential and more prone to boredom.

PLAN FOR PROGRESS

Don't wait until you sense you're in a rut – have an action plan to pre-empt boredom. Change some aspect of your training every two to three weeks. If you're new to running, it's good to build up your distances first rather than worrying about speed.

PATIENCE IS A VIRTUE...

Injury prevention should be foremost in your mind. Remember the '10 per cent rule': never increase distance, intensity or duration more than 10 per cent a week. Don't run two hard sessions back to back and always have at least one rest day per week.

LOG YOUR RUNS

A diary is a running essential: it's motivating and will highlight any weaknesses in your training. Note down how you felt during and after your run as well as distances and routes. If you're more techno-minded, take a look at page 82, for ways of electronically logging your runs.

RUN SMART

Aim to progress in flexible cycles, which will keep your programme energised, focused and interesting. Have a long-term goal alongside smaller manageable goals; for instance, aim to complete a 10k race in six months' time, but on a weekly basis concentrate on adding incremental distances and doing one new route every month. Use the SMART approach; make your goals Specific, Measurable, Achievable, Realistic and Time Framed.

MIX IT UP

Running is physically and mentally repetitive, so you need to factor in regular strength-building sessions and do other kinds of exercise you enjoy. For inspiration, take a look at our feature on cross-training on page 80, and gym wisdom on page 108.

Once you've built up your running and fitness, increase the intensity of your runs. Add two six-to-eight-minute bouts of running at a pace just beyond comfortable, recovering for one minute in between. Progress by increasing the number and/or length of this faster pace.

Q&A

WHY IS KEEPING TRACK OF MY HEART RATE SO USEFUL?

Whatever your level, you can use your heart rate to judge effort on your runs and, ultimately, to track your fitness. First, work out your resting heart rate (RHR) – how many times your heart beats each minute when you're resting. The stronger your heart, the lower it will be (because the heart pumps more blood with every beat) and the quicker you will return to your RHR after exercise. A normal rate is 70 beats per minute but it varies massively.

For more seasoned runners, it's also useful to work out your maximum heart rate (MHR) – the rate your heart beats every minute when it's working at full capacity. The easiest – though not totally accurate – method is to subtract your age from 220; if you're 30 your MHR will be 190. To gauge effort in your training, for example, if you need to work at 65 per cent, work out what your heart rate should be with the formula (MHR – RHR) x 65 per cent + RHR. If you're 30 and your resting heart rate is 70, your 65 per cent rate is 148bpm (120 x 65 per cent + 70).

If this is confusing, use a heart rate monitor, or 'rate of perceived exertion' (RPE) (when 0 = complete rest to 10 = maximal effort). During steady runs, aim for an RPE of around 3 or 4, and 6 or 7 during long speed sessions or hills.

STYLE CLINIC

Perfect your running technique to help boost your performance

Have you seen that episode of *Friends* when Phoebe demonstrates her unique approach to running? We all run in very different ways, and because our innate technique is hard-wired into us, it's impossible to define what is absolutely correct. This means there are no rigid rules you have to follow.

However, you can improve the way you run by optimising your movements to increase the efficiency of your running and minimise your risk of injury as a result. You can't transform your technique overnight; just try to be aware every time you run.

The most important thing you can do is remember to maintain a good, upright posture as you move (in other words, 'run tall') and to stay relaxed. If in doubt, ask a friend to monitor the way you run to help you streamline your posture.

HIPS & PELVIS
Keep your hips level and facing forwards. Don't stick your bum out too much: a pelvis that's tilted too far forward (an anterior tilt) is associated with tight or sore lower back muscles and overactive hamstrings.

SHOULDERS

Like your hips and chest, your shoulders should face forward and be level. Keep them broad and open, rather than hunched.

CHEST & TORSO

To maximise your breathing, keep your chest up and open. Avoid slouching to protect your posture and try not to lean forward or backward.

LEGS & ANKLES

As you run, imagine your legs working in circular motion from the hips and keep your ankles relaxed.

HEAD

Your head weighs somewhere between 4.5 and 5kg – around eight per cent of your body mass – so keep it in line with your spine and avoid bobbing and swaying your head or it will have a detrimental effect on your posture. Keep your jaw relaxed and your eyes focused on a point about 10 to 20 metres ahead of you.

KNEES

Avoid lifting your knees up too high in front of you. A bent knee has less resistance to rotation than a straight one but it allows the leg to swing through more efficiently from the hip. Keep knees slightly bent as your feet make contact with the ground.

FEET

Run with light feet, so they spring off the ground rather than pound it. They should point straight ahead and land directly under your hips. Transfer your weight evenly from one foot to the other, making sure all the time that you don't clench your toes. Increasing your length and stride rates will help to increase your speed.

ARMS & HANDS

How you hold your arms is in some ways instinctive, but try to keep your elbows bent at right angles and your forearms parallel to the ground. Don't swing your arms across your body or out to the sides. Keep your wrists and hands relaxed. You can use your arms to drive your body when you want to speed up.

Q&A

SHOULD I LAND HEEL OR TOE FIRST?

Some sports scientists say landing on your forefoot can help you avoid impact injuries and make you faster. But in reality, as with many hot running topics, there's no right or wrong, especially if you're a recreational runner rather than an athlete looking to break records.

Take note of how you run and make the key postural tweaks, but as long as you're fit and healthy, try not to obsess about how your feet land.

If you do get problems with your feet or knees, consider seeing a physiotherapist or running coach, who can assess your gait and posture with an expert eye.

**THE FLAT SURFACES AND
LARGE GRASS AREAS
OF PARKS ARE PERFECT**

PLAN YOUR ROUTES

Give your running some direction!

Nothing will wear away your enthusiasm for running more quickly than aimless ambling! Planning ahead is the key to a successful running routine. In very basic terms, plotting routes means you know your distances; it's not hard to deceive yourself that you're running further than you actually are, and conversely to under-estimate your achievements.

RUDIMENTARY ROUTES

The web and the corresponding boom in GPS gadgets and gizmos have made route planning effortlessly easy to do. So, if you'd rather not use an Ordnance Survey map, check out virtual plotters, such as www.runfinder.co.uk and www.mapmyrun.com, which enable you to log your training, save your favourite runs and swap ideas for routes with friends or other local runners.

If you're a novice, plot a linear and flat three-mile route; start off by doing half-mile sections and gradually add more as you gain confidence, varying the direction in which you run them.

Once you've established your credentials, you can start playing with distances and terrains. However, do keep one set route, which you can use as a progress check, trying to run it a little bit faster every time.

Consider the following factors when you're plotting your routes.

SAFETY

By now, you'll have read our safety advice, so do bear the messages in mind. Where possible, avoid head-on traffic, alleyways and dense, woody areas. Stick to open spaces with plenty of people but not so busy that your running is impeded.

TERRAIN

The flat surfaces and large grass areas of parks are perfect for running, particularly if you're a beginner. But do explore new gradients and terrains as you develop, to make running more interesting and challenge your body in new ways. Trails and canal towpaths are a great step up.

SIGHTS

Make sure your routes are visually stimulating – even in cities as densely populated and hectic as London, there are pockets of greenery.

SPECIAL FEATURES

Do you need frequent loo breaks? Are you scared of dogs and find your local park a bit too stressful? Do you want to stop for coffee with your running buddy after your run? Make sure your routes are tailored to you so they're as enjoyable as possible.

Q&A
SHOULD I WORRY ABOUT AIR POLLUTION?

When you exercise intensively, you breathe harder, so in theory you are more susceptible to air pollution, particularly if you're an urban runner. But when it comes to your lungs, the benefits of running far outweigh any disadvantages.

Take some sensible precautions: the air tends to be clearer in the early mornings, so schedule your outdoor sessions first thing, especially if the weather is hot and still, and stay away from busy roads.

Keep an eye on www.airquality.co.uk for up-to-date reports, and if you suffer with a respiratory condition such as asthma, speak to your GP before you embark on a running programme.

STAY

Keep your enthusiasm firing on all cylinders!

MOTIVATED

As well as making gradual changes to your weekly routine and progressing your running, try some of our other strategies to maximise your motivation levels.

FIND SOME COMPANY

If you don't fancy joining a club or you just don't feel you can make the commitment, enlist a friend to run with you. They should be around the same ability as you, but try to choose someone who is energised and can push you when needed. Approach your runs as you would any engagement – plan ahead to find a time to suit you both and decide what kind of run to do.

USE MUSIC

Although there are safety issues about listening to music, provided you're running in a safe environment such as a park or on the treadmill, it can give you a tremendous lift. Studies at Brunel University have revealed music lowers your perception of effort and can trick your mind into feeling less fatigued during a workout.

ASK FOR EXPERT ADVICE

Find yourself a coach (visit www. exerciseregister.org) or book a dedicated running break to fine-tune your technique and access advice that's tailored specifically to your needs, aims and abilities. If you don't have the funds or inclination, there's always virtual training: take a look at our feature on technology on pages 82–83.

GET RACE-PREPARED

Nothing will boost your commitment to your programme more than the prospect of a race – and we guarantee the atmosphere on the day will remind you why you got into running! To ease yourself in gently, choose a fun 5k women-only race or a fancy dress event. Have a look at our race pages on 124–127 for ideas.

Q&A

IS IT OK TO RUN DURING MY PERIOD?

There is some evidence that professional athletes are affected by the menstrual cycle and more prone to injury at certain times but as a recreational runner, there's definitely no reason why you can't continue to exercise through PMS and your actual period. In fact, it's actually a brilliant way to help take your mind off some of the symptoms, and will often help physically relieve some of them too.
This is because after exercise our bodies are flushed with feel-good, pain-relieving chemicals called endorphins. Take things easy if you're feeling off-colour, always remember to warm up and stretch adequately and use over-the-counter medication such as ibuprofen or paracetamol to deal with any abdominal cramps.

NO EXCUSES!

It's easy to talk yourself out of a run. These tips tackle your excuses.

■ I DON'T HAVE TIME…

You need a change of mindset. See the time you set aside to exercise as an investment rather than a chore. Feeling energised, refreshed and upbeat after a run will help you achieve more in the rest of your life. Focus on quality, not quantity, in your running when you're short of time – do quick bursts of running at a pace slightly above comfortable to boost your cardio system. Finally, can you crowbar a quick run into your lunch break or run all or part of the way to work?

■ I'M NOT ACHIEVING ANYTHING…

Are your goals too hard to reach? Concentrate on manageable, bite-size achievements rather than radical, life-changing experiences. Keep a diary of your runs so whenever you're feeling deflated, you can look back and be enthused by your progress. If you took up running for weight loss, try to focus on how you're feeling and the fit of your clothes, rather than your weight.

■ IT'S HURTING…

Have you read through our technique and injury features? Are you experiencing mild discomfort or genuine pain? If it's the latter, see a physiotherapist or sports therapist who'll help get to the root of the problem. Don't push your body too much. Respect your planned rest days and schedule in cross-training, such as swimming and resistance work, to rejuvenate your mind and strengthen your body.

FOCUS ON RUNNING QUALITY NOT QUANTITY WHEN YOU'RE TIME POOR

JOIN THE CLUB

Solo running is fantastic but sometimes you can't beat a bit of company

Many people have an image of running clubs as being the preserve of super-svelte, speedy pros, but in fact they have never been so inclusive. Although some will require you to have basic running experience – you will have to be able to run for a certain length of time without stopping – most cater for all levels.

WHY JOIN?

In many ways, clubs are ideal for beginners since running in a group is motivating and you'll meet expert runners who can pass on advice.

➤ The support of your fellow members can get you through the pain barrier and keep you going on long or tough runs.

➤ Running in a group will get you used to the sensation of having people around you at a race and buttress your confidence if you feel unsafe or self-conscious on your own.

➤ Most clubs offer technique and drill training sessions, which are much easier to do when there's someone else measuring and/or timing you.

➤ Clubs are sociable – you can join in social events.

➤ Running in a group will increase your competitive drive, without you even realising it.

➤ From race-day advice to the best local runs and where to get a sports massage, clubs are heaving with knowledgeable and helpful people.

➤ There are financial benefits too. Compared to the gym, club membership fees are low and most also offer reduced race entry fees and discounts at local running shops.

Q&A

WHAT IS STITCH ND HOW CAN I PREVENT GETTING IT?

Sadly, no one has fathomed why side stitches occur. However, the good news is there are plenty of ways to prevent them. Avoid eating a heavy meal in the two to four hours before a run; stick to small, simple snacks and don't gulp down too much water. If a stitch does strike, slow down to a walk, press into the spot and massage it until some of the discomfort has lifted.

TYPES OF RUNNING CLUB

Make sure you do your research; before committing to anything, check the club fits in with your aims and also your lifestyle.

■ PERFORMANCE-FOCUSED

If you're a serious runner or looking for focused race preparation, check out the athletics clubs close to you, via www.uka.org.uk

■ AMATEUR AND COMMUNITY-BASED

Looking for a relaxed, friendly group where the focus is on recreation rather than competition? Take a peek at www.runinengland.co.uk or www.jogscotland.org.uk – networks of accessible running collectives that welcome any gender, age and ability.

■ SOCIABLE

Perhaps you've moved to a new area and want to make new friends or you're newly single? Or you think the pub jaunt afterwards is more important than the run itself (known as 'hashing'). Then www.meetup.com is a good place to start looking for a club with like-minded people.

GROUND FORCE

Vary your running environment to get maximum benefits

One of the key messages we hope we're getting across is that mixing things up can keep it interesting – and this goes for what's underfoot, too. Swapping the type of surfaces you run on will relieve boredom, enhance your enjoyment of running and, most importantly, help prevent injuries.

Soft, uneven ground is far more forgiving on the joints than hard surfaces such as concrete or asphalt, but it also challenges the muscles of the lower body more. A study at Liverpool John Moores University also found off-road running demands a greater range of movement at the hips and knees, in order to lift the feet higher to clear long grass, puddles or obstacles – increasing the activity of the hamstrings, quadriceps and hip flexors. Each surface and terrain has pros and cons…

ROADS AND PAVEMENTS

Flat, navigable and accessible, plus you can use features such as lampposts and benches for stretches and as markers for speed training. However, surfaces such as concrete and asphalt create the most shock to your joints and these places can be busy, so divert into green spaces when possible. Approach cambers, pot-holes and kerbs with caution.

GRASSLAND

Park grassland, golf courses and football pitches are soft and joint-friendly, but challenging enough to test your muscles. Take care when it's wet and slippery, especially if you have weak ankles, and avoid running in long grass if you suffer with hay fever.

RUNNING TRACKS

These are reasonably forgiving on the body and, because of the markings, great for speed training and technique sessions. On the downside, they can be boring and aren't the most welcoming of places for newbies. Always check access, as you may need to join a club to use your local track.

WOODLAND TRAILS

Softer ground and ever-changing environs make this terrain a great choice for runners. Woodland trails can sometimes be muddy, unless they benefit from a covering of wood chip, and you'll probably have to share them with cyclists and dog walkers. Look out for natural hazards such as tree roots, rocks and large branches. Start with manicured trails such as public footpaths around a lake, then work up to more demanding ground.

CLOTHING: Casall, www.casallshara.com; Sweaty Betty, www.sweatybetty.com; Asics, www.asics.com

SOFT GROUND IS MORE FORGIVING ON JOINTS THAN CONCRETE

ADVENTUROUS RUNNING TRENDS

- **NIGHT RUNNING:** head torch essential.
- **TOWER RUNNING:** head up tall manmade structures at top speed.
- **BACKWARDS RUNNING:** check out www.reverserunning.com.
- **BAREFOOT RUNNING:** for the brave and strong of foot.
- **DOG RUNNING:** recruit a canine pal. **See** www.cani-cross.co.uk.

HILLS

A study from the University of Georgia in Greece confirms muscle activation is greater in hill running than on the flat, particularly in the thighs, gluteals and calves. Battling against gravity increases the cardiovascular effort, too. But hills are tough, especially for beginners, and descending can put stress on the knees and test your quadriceps.

SAND

Beaches are visually stimulating and great for building leg strength, but the soft sand provides a higher risk of Achilles tendon injury. Tilts and cambers can also send the body out of alignment. It's best to do this only occasionally.

TREADMILL

There are advantages (all-year-round accessibility, pre-set programmes, heart rate monitoring, lower-impact) and disadvantages (the 'pull' underneath your feet, the lack of environmental factors that challenge you) to using a treadmill. See pages 62–63 for treadmill tips. Use one wisely from time to time, but go outdoors to run as much as possible.

WEATHER-PROOF YOUR PROGRAMME

How to enjoy running, whatever the season

An ideal running day is one that's dry, warm and not too breezy or sunny, but given how unpredictable the UK weather is, it's best not to limit your options. A mindset shift is vital if you're going to be a regular outdoor runner – you need to accept the weather won't always be great, but you can adjust your routes and sessions to suit the conditions – even during the darkest, dullest days of winter. As well as changing your attitude, make sure you get your kit right too.

OUTLOOK: COLD

> Dress in layers, so you can add or discard clothing, according to the improving or worsening conditions. Start with a base layer – ideally a long-sleeved but breathable, close-fitting top. Depending on the temperature, you may want a second layer and a jacket, or just one or the other. And look on the figurative bright side – according to some studies, the number of calories you burn increases by up to 12 per cent during outdoor workouts in cold weather.

> Always wear a hat and gloves (or mittens if it's really cold). If you don't like gloves, tops with extra-long sleeves or thumb loops are a good compromise, enabling you to free your hands once they warm up enough.

> Temperatures are at their lowest in the early morning and late evening, so you may want to avoid activity at these times.

> Allow more time for your warm-up, to ensure your muscles are thoroughly prepared for running and to get accustomed to breathing in cold air. This is particularly important for anyone with exercise-induced asthma or other respiratory problems – try wearing a scarf and breathing through the fabric for the first few minutes to warm the air before it hits your lungs. Once your session is finished, don't hang around stretching in the cold – get inside and get warm!

OUTLOOK: WIND

> As much as 80 per cent of heat lost from the body is due to wind chill so if your main concern is to block out

the wind, and you only need shower-resistant rather than waterproof protection, select a jacket made from Windstopper Soft Shell or Active Shell.

OUTLOOK: RAIN

> In addition to a jacket, a hat with a brim can be your best friend during a rainy run. When it comes to shoes, choose a pair with a Gore-Tex upper.

> Put in your contact lenses rather than wearing glasses, otherwise you'll be constantly stopping to wipe them.

> Keep gadgets such as your mobile phone and iPod in a waterproof bag or pocket.

> As soon as you get home, remove your wet clothes and put your trainers out to dry.

OUTLOOK: FOG AND/ OR DARKNESS

> Bright yellow or orange kit will make you stand out on dull days, but at night, reflective panels or strips are visible from a greater distance than bright colours. For maximum effect, wear reflective gear on your 'moving parts' (the arms and legs), rather than on your trunk.

> Stick to routes you're familiar with in daylight, so you're aware of missing paving stones, slippery drain covers, rutted roads and collision hazards, such as railings or bollards.

OUTLOOK: ICE

> Shoes with good traction are crucial on slippery or icy terrain – check the bottom of the shoe (outsole) for 'lugs' that will provide essential grip.

> If you're doing a timed loop or interval session, avoid a course with tight bends or turns that might have you skidding out of control.

OUTLOOK: SUN

> If you can, avoid training when the sun is at its strongest (between 11am and 3pm) and stick to shady routes.

> UV exposure is the number one cause of premature skin ageing and can also cause skin cancer, so protect yourself. Cosset your skin with SPF protection (30+ is advisable), and choose a sport-specific brand. Don't forget the back and sides of your neck, temples and ears.

> Buy a sports visor or cap and a pair of lightweight sunglasses to protect your eyes even on overcast summer days – the sun can still be damaging. If you're particularly sun-sensitive, consider clothing made from wicking fabric that has inbuilt SPF protection.

OUTLOOK: HOT AND HUMID

> If possible, limit your training to the coolest hours of the day – early mornings and late evenings. Otherwise, the treadmill at your air-conditioned gym may be a more comfortable option.

> Sweating is an essential bodily process, but it can lead to blisters and chafing. Don lightweight, light-coloured, moisture-wicking fabrics, including your socks, and if necessary, use a sweat-resistant lube for trouble spots, such as under your bra straps.

> Hydration is paramount; if you don't replace the fluids you've sweated out, your core temperature will rise, your cardio system will have to work harder and you'll tire quickly. Drink plenty before you leave and at regular intervals during your run.

UP TO 80 PER CENT OF BODY HEAT LOSS IS DUE TO WIND CHILL

COLD COMFORT

Given your body requires additional energy to combat the effects of air temperature, wind and rain, it's important to give some thought to winter fuelling. If you're doing anything but the shortest of sessions, don't run on an empty stomach – cold days mean you need to insulate yourself before you set off (another of the upsides of winter running). And don't forget to drink on the run – you might not notice it so much, but you're still sweating and need to replace lost fluid.

CLOTHING: Sweaty Betty, www.sweatybetty.com

TREADMILL TRAINING

Get the most out of your gym sessions

I t's often seen as a poor relation to outdoor running, but using a treadmill has many advantages too. Running machines give you access to hills and challenging terrain at the touch of a button, plus they can accurately monitor distance, calorie burn and heart rate. And they're not subject to the vagaries of the weather or season, so you can get in your runs even in the depths of an icy winter or stifling summer. The gym is also a whole lot safer than the dark city streets for solo runners and since the treadmill belt is also far less stressful on the body than concrete, it's a good option if you're injury-prone or recovering from a particular problem.

But these advantages have a flipside. Without added environmental factors such as wind and uneven terrain, and with a conveyor-like 'pulling' effect on the feet, treadmills can make running less physically challenging, thereby limiting the possible benefits. The flat, monotonous and soft surface isn't great for building stability in your knee and ankle joints. The view isn't so great either; you don't need us to tell you the gym environment is far less visually stimulating than your local park or green space.

MAXIMISE THE HEALTH BENEFITS...

Do try to get outdoors as much as possible, but when you're using a treadmill, remember these top tips.

As a general rule, always set the incline to at least one per cent to match the demands of the outdoors; research from Brighton University shows having the belt on a slight incline compensates for the lack of wind resistance and varied terrain that make running in the 'real world' more challenging.

Avoid continuously looking down at the belt or machine controls. Keep your posture, as you would outdoors – run tall, looking straight ahead. Use the mirrors at the gym for assessing your running posture and technique.

Don't just plod along at the same speed and gradient. Make the most of the machine's features, such as pre-set sessions, hills and varied pace to add variety, or create your own interval sessions, using distance or time – take a look at page 78 for ideas. Race a friend for extra motivation.

Always enter your age and weight correctly, so you get accurate readings for calorie burn and heart rate. Ask your gym if you can borrow a chest strap, so the heart-rate measurements are precise.

Since you don't have to worry about safety concerns such as traffic, listen to your favourite motivating music to power your running and help beat boredom.

INJURY CLINIC

Keep your body in top working order

R unning is incredibly accessible, but that doesn't mean you won't feel some physical discomfort. At some point, all runners will encounter pain or an injury of some sort, but provided you stay aware and take a balanced approach to running, you can prevent a short-term problem turning into a chronic issue.

COMMON GRIPES

SHIN SPLINTS

This is a broad term for pain along the tibia in the lower leg. The most common cause is medial tibial traction periostitis, an inflammatory condition brought on by muscles of the lower leg pulling on the bone.

PREVENT: Excessive pronation is a major factor, so make sure you wear the right footwear (see page 30).

TREAT: It's essential to find and eliminate the cause. A physiotherapist or another sports medicine professional can help you take the necessary steps: changing your shoes, strength training and cross-training will help prevent a recurrence.

ACHILLES TENDONITIS

Your Achilles tendon, which runs from your large calf muscles to your heel, gives you the power to push off when you run. It's an overuse injury but overpronation is a factor.

PREVENT: Don't push yourself too much, try to vary running surfaces and make sure you're wearing the right footwear for your gait. Ensure you include calf stretches in your strength programme.

TREAT: Pain relief, rest and physiotherapy are essential. Heel pads in your shoes and compression bandaging may also help.

RUNNER'S KNEE

The impact of running on the knees is an enduring debate that shows no sign of being resolved. Recent research at the University of California suggested it can increase risk of osteoarthritis in middle-aged knees. But for every piece of negative research, there's a positive nugget of news. Another long-term study at Stanford University tracked nearly 1,000 runners and healthy non-runners over 21 years and found the runners' knees were no more or less healthy. In truth, it's only bad for your knees if you have bad technique.

Pain on the outside of the knee is caused by inflammation and tightness in the iliotibial band (ITB), the connective tissue that runs down the outside of the leg from the hip to just below the knee. It may be due to poor running technique, weak gluteals (bottom muscles), tight hip flexor muscles or worn-out or inappropriate shoes.

PREVENT: Regularly stretch your hip flexors and ITB by massaging a tennis ball firmly along the side of your leg. Do step-ups to build up the gluteals.

TREAT: First, rest and ice the sore area for eight minutes, twice a day. When the pain has gone, run little and often.

Q&A

MY TOENAIL HAS GONE BLACK. WHAT HAS CAUSED THIS AND HOW CAN I PREVENT IT HAPPENING AGAIN?

It sounds as if your toe has suffered a subungual haematoma. This usually happens when your shoe is too tight and the big toe (or nail) is pushed down into the nail bed, which then becomes inflamed and bruised. The painful build-up of blood behind the nail eventually goes away on its own, but a doctor or chiropodist can put a sterile pin into the nail to release the pressure if it's really bothering you.

To prevent it happening again, cut your nails short and straight across and make sure your shoes fit properly. Remember, your running shoes should always be a size bigger than your regular shoes, to allow your feet to slide forward and swell.

TOP TIP

Remember the RICE principle: rest, ice, compression and elevation should be the first treatment for sprains and strains. Seek professional medical attention for serious injuries, such as suspected fractures.

Q&A
SHOULD I RUN IF I HAVE A COLD?

It depends on two things: the severity of the cold and the type of symptoms you have. If your symptoms are from the neck upwards (such as runny nose, headache or mild sore throat) and you don't feel too bad, a short, easy-paced run should do you no harm and, in fact, might make you feel better. If, however, your symptoms are below the neck – chesty cough, aching limbs – avoid any training until you're completely well. Once you do go back to training, don't rush things or you may leave yourself susceptible to another bug.

PLANTAR FASCIITIS

Overuse of the plantar fascia, the thick tendon running from under the heel to the front of the foot, causes pain that is most often felt under the heel, on the inside. The most common cause is tight calf muscles and an abnormal running gait.

PREVENT: Ensure you're wearing the right kind of shoes and make sure you regularly stretch your calves and feet. Use a tennis ball under your sole as a massage tool.

TREAT: Use the RICE principle and rest. See a physio for advice on footwear, heel pads and arch supports. Take regular pain relief such as ibuprofen and paracetamol.

TIGHT HIP FLEXORS

These muscles at the very top of the front of your legs are a real trouble spot because, as you run, they repeatedly contract and shorten. They can be painful in their own right and lead to back pain, because tightness can cause the pelvis to tilt forwards.

PREVENT: Always include hip stretches in your strength routine, including lunges and a post-run stretch. Use a tennis ball to massage away pain.

TREAT: Rest and use pain relief, including cool packs. See a physiotherapist who can provide immediate treatment and long-term management.

HAMSTRING STRAIN

Your hamstrings, the muscles at the back of your thighs, play a key role when you're running so it's no surprise they can be vulnerable. You may feel tightness and a sudden sharp pain at the back of the leg and the back of the knee too. It can be caused by muscle imbalance: poor technique (a pelvis that's tilted too far forward and overworks your hamstrings), weak quadriceps (the muscles at the front of your thighs) and lack of flexibility.

PREVENT: Make sure you always warm up and don't over-exert yourself. Backward running and flexibility exercise such as yoga may also help improve any imbalances. Be careful you're not overextending your legs as you run.

TREAT: Regular ice packs and physiotherapy.

SPRAINED ANKLE

This occurs when the ligaments attached to the ankle are overstretched or twisted. It's caused by a combination of weak ankles and uneven terrain. Sprains vary in severity from mild to a full or part ligament tear.

PREVENT: Cross-train and strength-train to build up strength in your ankles and also to improve your balance and coordination. Yoga is particularly good. Wear supportive footwear and take care on uneven surfaces.

TREAT: Apply the RICE method, rest and seek professional advice for serious or recurrent problems.

KEY INJURY PREVENTION TIPS

- Build up your mileage and effort gradually.
- Wear the right kit.
- Watch your posture.
- Sandwich your long runs between rest or easy training days.
- Vary your running surfaces.
- Cross-train and factor in strength-building sessions.
- Eat well and stay hydrated.
- Always warm up and stretch thoroughly afterwards.
- See a health professional if pain lingers for more than a day or two, or comes on during the run itself.
- Get regular sports massages.
- Listen to your body!

5K PLAN

Personal trainer **Cat Dugdale** helps you run your first 5k event

QUICK TIPS

• Remember to warm up
and stretch after each session,
using our guides on pages 34–41.

• At least twice a week, find the time
for our strength-building exercises on
pages 112–123. You can tag them on to the
end of one of your run sessions. Test your
fitness at the beginning and the end
of the programme.

• Stick to a steady pace and
a flat, navigable terrain.

WEEK	MONDAY	TUESDAY	WEDNESDAY	THURSDAY	FRIDAY	SATURDAY	SUNDAY
1	Run 2 minutes, walk 2 minutes x 6	REST	Cross-train	30-minute power walk	REST	Run 2 minutes, walk 2 minutes x 6	REST
2	Run 5 minutes, walk 2 minutes x 4	REST	Cross-train	30-minute power walk	REST	Run 5 minutes, walk 2 minutes x 4	REST
3	Run 1km, walk 2 minutes x 3	REST	Cross-train	Run 15 minutes, walk 5 minutes, run 5 minutes	REST and reward yourself	Run 1km, walk 2 minutes x 3	REST
4	Run 2km, walk 2 minutes x 2	REST	Cross-train	Run 15 minutes, walk 5 minutes, run 5 minutes	REST	Run 2km, walk 2 minutes x 2	REST
5	Run 3km	REST	Cross-train	Run 20 minutes, walk 5 minutes, run 5 minutes	REST	Run 3km	REST
6	Run 4km	REST and reward yourself	Cross-train	Run 20 minutes, walk 5 minutes, run 5 minutes	REST	Run 5km	CELEBRATE!

5K PLAN

10K PLAN

Personal trainer **Cat Dugdale** helps you run your first 10k event

QUICK TIPS

• Remember to warm up and stretch after each session, using our guides on pages 34–41.

• At least twice a week, find the time for our strength-building exercises on pages 112–123. You can tag them on to the end of one of your run sessions. Test your fitness at the beginning and the end of the programme.

• This plan includes some entry-level speed work and a couple of time trials, where you'll need to run as fast as is comfortable and time the runs. Now you're gaining experience you can also think about varying your terrain.

WEEK	MONDAY	TUESDAY	WEDNESDAY	THURSDAY	FRIDAY	SATURDAY	SUNDAY
1	Run 2 minutes, walk 1 minute x 10	*REST*	Cross-train	30-minute power walk	*REST*	Run 3km	*REST*
2	Run 3km	*REST*	Cross-train	30-second sprint, 1-minute walk x 8	*REST*	Run 5km	*REST*
3	Run 5km	*REST*	Cross-train	30-second sprint, 1-minute walk x 8	*REST*	Run 5km time trial	*REST*
4	*REST* and reward yourself	*REST*	Cross-train	Run 40 minutes comfy pace	*REST*	Run 6km	*REST*
5	Run 5km	*REST*	Cross-train	Run 1 minute fast paced, 1 minute light jog x 8	*REST* and massage	Run 7km	*REST*
6	Run 5km	*REST*	Cross-train	Run 1 minute fast paced, 1 minute light jog x 8	*REST*	Run 8km	*REST*
7	Run 5km	*REST*	Cross-train	30-second sprint, 1-minute walk x 8	*REST* and massage	Run 8km	*REST*
8	Run 5km	*REST*	Cross-train	30-second sprint, 1-minute walk x 8	*REST* and reward yourself	Run 10km time trial	*CELEBRATE!*

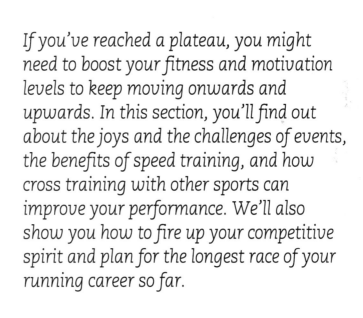

RUN AHEAD

If you've reached a plateau, you might need to boost your fitness and motivation levels to keep moving onwards and upwards. In this section, you'll find out about the joys and the challenges of events, the benefits of speed training, and how cross training with other sports can improve your performance. We'll also show you how to fire up your competitive spirit and plan for the longest race of your running career so far.

CLOTHING: Nike, www.nikestore.com; American Apparel, www.americanapparel.co.uk; Shock Absorber, www.shockabsorber.co.uk; Sweaty Betty, www.sweatybetty.com; Asics, www.asics.com; Brooks, www.brooksrunning.co.uk

THERE'S NOTHING LIKE A GOAL TO SUPER-CHARGE YOUR RUNNING

TAKE IT FURTHER

Discover new ways to take your running up another level

Even if you don't think of yourself as ambitious, since you started running you've probably discovered a competitive streak you've never seen before. You may not want to break records but it's human nature to want to get better. Here's how to capitalise on your hunger...

RUN FASTER

Now you have a good basic level of fitness, it's time to start pushing your speed. Weekly interval training, even on a treadmill, will help your body move more economically and boost your cardiovascular fitness. Research from the University of Vermont found 40-second intervals at near-maximal pace (interspersed with 20-second jogs) can help raise your aerobic capacity by an impressive 11 per cent. Turn to page 78 to find out more.

RUN FURTHER

As well as improving your endurance, running longer distances will get you used to the sensation of being on your feet for protracted periods – essential if you're planning a half or full marathon.

RUN WITH PASSION

There's nothing like a goal to super-charge your running. Commit yourself to a race in a few months' time that's significantly different to anything you've done before. And to put real fire in your belly, find a cause that inspires you and get fundraising!

RUN LONGER... AND SHORTER

Sticking with the 10 per cent rule, increase your weekly mileage. As your body adapts, this will help improve your basic pace. But also do shorter runs at a faster pace to improve your leg turnover (steps per minute) and teach your body to process lactic acid more efficiently.

RUN ASSISTED

Check out your local running groups for a boost to your training. Now running is a firm fixture in your life, it might be worth investing in some running gadgetry – take a look at our feature on pages 82–83 for ideas.

RUN HARDER

It's hard, but hill work will elevate your cardiovascular fitness and strength. Remember to keep an upright posture, use your arms to power and take 'baby steps'. If you live in a flat area, use a treadmill to replicate steep gradients.

RUN CONFIDENTLY

Don't underestimate the power of positive thought! Professional athletes learn to banish a fear of failure and you should follow suit.

Q&A

WHAT IS THE BEST TECHNIQUE FOR RUNNING DOWNHILL?

Use a technique that will limit the impact and make the most of the benefits. The fact you aren't working against gravity allows you to travel faster, increasing leg turnover (the speed at which your legs move). Over time, this can translate into faster leg turnover on the flat – which is why it's often used in sprint training. The problem is, many of us don't take advantage of this 'free' speed, attempting to hold back or 'brake' as we descend, not only missing out on the benefits, but also putting a lot of stress on the thigh muscles and knees. Look at the path ahead, not down at the ground, and stay relaxed – don't tense up or 'grip' with the thighs. Use your arms for balance by taking them wider and take small, fast strides. On shallower slopes, try to land on your forefoot rather than your heel. Don't lean back. You should be at a slight forward-leaning angle to the hill so your feet land under your centre of gravity.

TRAINING
DRILLS

Hone your technique and
improve your performance
with these targeted sessions

properly and never push yourself beyond your capabilities; you should feel challenged, but never nauseous or in pain. If possible, buddy up with a friend – it'll make measuring and timing things less stressful and also keep you motivated. There are many training methods but the following are the most common.

FARTLEK

Meaning 'speed play' in Swedish – a Fartlek session comprises bursts of intense activity and recovery. Sessions normally last around 45 minutes, and you should be working at 60 to 80 per cent of your maximum heart rate (see page 47 for explanation) during the high-octane portions. It's fun, less structured than intervals and therefore better for beginners, as the point is to let your surroundings dictate what you're doing. So, for instance, you can use benches and lampposts as markers.

TRY: Don't structure it too much at first; just say to yourself 'I will run fast, as far as that tree' then recover with a light jog and pick another goal. Take a friend along so you can alternate who calls out the next marker. Once you're used to the principles, time your bursts. For instance, warm up with a

Steady runs are the bread and butter of training. But once you have some sound experience and good aerobic fitness, you can start introducing more varied sessions in your programme. Even for recreational runners, these offer huge gains. They're a break from the norm and make training, especially for an event, more interesting.

Speed training, in particular, is energising and an economical use of your time. Regular sessions can also make you fitter and faster by challenging your body in new ways – and are therefore a great injury-prevention strategy.

Apply the general principles of training to your sessions. Ease into it – just as you slowly developed your running from walk-run-walk-run outings, gradually increase your effort in your specialised training. Always warm up and cool down

Q&A
WHAT IS A RECOVERY RUN?

It's a slow, light run to help your body recover from the hard grind of training and teach it how to move when it's fatigued (as it will be in the closing stages of a marathon). It's only really necessary if you run four or more times a week and are a seriously committed runner. Tailor the distance and speed according to your capabilities.

steady jog for 10 minutes, run hard for three minutes, walk for one, then repeat it all six times.

LONG, SLOW RUNS

This is an essential part of your weekly programme if you're building up for a big event, particularly a half or full marathon. Pushing your distances will get you used to being on your feet and will increase your muscle strength, endurance and aerobic fitness. However, it can be boring, and obviously time-consuming!

TRY: The distance depends on what you're training for; if you're working towards a half-marathon, it may be nine to 11 miles. Try to concentrate on maintaining an easy pace; you should be running at a speed that still enables you to have a conversation, which equates to about one to three minutes per mile slower than your 10k pace.

HILL TRAINING

By now you should know about the benefits of conquering some steeper gradients. You can vary the kinds of hills you use in your training – short, steep hills or ones that take no longer than 30 seconds to scale will test your anaerobic fitness (see Q&A below), medium hills of say 30 to 90 seconds' worth of running build muscular endurance, as do long hills (anything over 90 seconds).

TRY: You can try hill training on a treadmill – a great idea if you live in a particularly flat place – as it makes it much easier to gauge gradients. Warm up and then, using a hill (or treadmill setting) of three to five per cent gradient, do a set of intervals of anything from 30 to 250 metres long. Recover with a light jog and return to the foot of the hill if you're outdoors. Do four or five intervals and gradually build up reps and reduce recovery.

THRESHOLD TRAINING

Lactate threshold (LT) is a term that regularly crops up in running. It's the point at which lactic acid (a by-product of burning carbohydrates for energy) accumulates in the muscles faster than it can be flushed out. This creates a highly acidic environment, which hampers muscular contraction. The value of training just below the threshold is it teaches the body to clear lactic acid more efficiently (ultimately raising LT) and to tolerate its presence.

TRY: Your threshold pace should be outside your comfort zone but manageable. You probably won't be able to hold a long conversation but your breathing shouldn't be ragged or uncontrolled. This is roughly 75 to 90 per cent of your maximum heart rate (MHR), depending on your level of experience. If you've done races before, your LT pace should be slower than 10km pace but faster than half-marathon. Try running for five minutes at your LT, then recover for one minute. Repeat four times. You can gradually increase the duration of your LT intervals and decrease the actual number that you do.

INTERVALS

Interval training is a more structured version of Fartlek. You do periods of high-speed/intensity running followed by periods of recovery. With intervals, you need to time and map your distances with more precision. The intervals will help your body use oxygen more efficiently. Try interval training only if you're an advanced and experienced runner.

INTERVAL TRAINING HELPS YOUR BODY USE OXYGEN EFFICIENTLY

TRY: Again, the treadmill is a useful tool for intervals. There are lots of types of interval training – shorter, higher-intensity intervals (repetitions of 60 seconds to three minutes at 90 per cent of MHR) help you prepare for shorter races such as 5ks, while tempo intervals are longer (between 90 seconds and 10 minutes or between 400m and two miles at 85 to 95 per cent of MHR) and help you prepare for longer events.

Do the intense sections at the higher end of your MHR. For shorter intervals, try 10 reps of 60-second effort, with 60 seconds' recovery in between. For longer ones, try three reps of eight-minute intervals, with two minutes' recovery in between.

Q&A
WHAT'S THE DIFFERENCE BETWEEN ANAEROBIC AND AEROBIC EXERCISE?

Aerobic exercise uses oxygen. Think swimming, cycling and walking – anything that gets the heart and lungs pumping. Anaerobic exercise doesn't use oxygen but relies on the body's own resources for fuel, namely glycogen, which is stored carbohydrate in your muscle. This is because anaerobic exercise requires you to work at such an intensity the body can't deliver enough oxygen to the working muscles. It tends to be shorter and sharper than aerobic exercise – examples include sprinting and weight training. A balance of the two types of exercise is necessary to make you a strong, versatile runner.

TECHNIQUE DRILLS

By isolating aspects of running, you can scan your technique, correct any glaring flaws and improve your running efficiency. Always warm up and start by covering 30 metres doing the exercises below, then repeat the exercises a couple of times. Build the distance up to 60m and increase the reps over time. Try a technique session every week, tagged on the end or mix it into one of your runs. Here are a few examples...

> HIGH KNEES
Using a short stride, raise your knees as high as possible so you're almost bouncing on your toes. Don't lean back. This is great for working your core strength.

> QUICK FEET
This exercise will, over time, help make your running steps lighter and shorter. Simply cover your distance in small, fast steps without much knee-lift.

> HEEL KICKS
Using a short stride, flick your heels back up towards your bum. Try to keep your upper body (including the top of your legs) still. This will work your gluteals and improve your stride.

> CROSSOVERS
A great exercise for improving balance. Move sideways, alternately crossing one leg in front of the other.

CROSS FIT

Including other types of exercise in your training can balance your body and improve your running

Find time in your exercise schedule for cross-training – complementary sports and activities – to balance your mind and body.

Running is, by its very nature, physically repetitive, so challenging your body in other ways will prevent something known in sports science as 'pattern overload' and lower your risk of injury. Cross-training can boost your non-running muscles and give your running muscles a respite – especially important if you're recovering from a niggle of some kind – and help keep things interesting. Aerobic exercise such as swimming and dancing will also elevate your cardiovascular fitness.

The amount of cross-training you should do depends on how much you run, whether you're carrying an injury and, of course, how much spare time you have! That said, aim for at least two non-running sessions a week.

YOGA AND PILATES

Holistic forms of exercise are a great outlet for stress; a chance to bliss-out from everyday life and the rigours of running. They're also fabulous for working the nooks and crannies of your body. They'll open up the hips, expand the chest, strengthen your ankles and elongate the spine, all of which are beneficial for your running. Plus, they improve core strength and co-ordination.

SWIMMING

A fantastic, relaxing non-weight-bearing rest for your joints, swimming boosts your heart and lungs, and challenges your upper body (which gets neglected in running). Vary your strokes for maximum benefits and why not have a go at aquarobics or water running with a flotation aid for added interest?

STRENGTH TRAINING

We've included a run-specific strength routine on pages 112–123. In addition, it's worthwhile factoring in a whole-body resistance (working against your body weight) or weights (using free-weights or machines) session in your weekly schedule. Great for ironing out imbalances, boosting your core and balance and improving overall muscular strength.

CYCLING OR SPINNING

Like swimming, cycling will help boost your cardio fitness. It's also great for lower-body muscular strength, especially in your quadriceps and gluteals so it complements running. Plus it's low impact so can be good if you're recovering from injury.

ROWING

This is another great low-impact, cardiovascular activity that's particularly good for strengthening the hips, gluteals and upper body. If you use the rowing machine in your local gym, make sure an instructor shows you how to adopt the correct posture and technique.

SKIPPING

Forever synonymous with the playground, skipping is the ideal addition to a grown-up running programme. It's adaptable, inexpensive, a great cardio workout and calorie burner, plus it can help build muscle tone in your lower body and give your bones a boost, too. Skipping also demands lightning reflexes so regular sessions will do wonders for your co-ordination. Integrate into pre-run warm-ups or gym sessions.

Q&A

WHAT'S CORE STRENGTH AND HOW CAN IT HELP MY RUNNING?

Your core muscles are deep within your abdominals and back, attached to the spine and pelvis. They are an essential source of stability and power in your body, even though most of us would be hard pressed to explain where they are! To activate them, imagine you're trying to stop yourself peeing, and pull your belly button towards your spine.

Core strength is integral to running because it'll help you refine your posture, stay balanced and take pressure off your spine. Your core acts as an internal corset that keeps your pelvis stable – without it, your pelvis can tip forward and your hamstrings and hip flexors won't function properly. There's no reason why you can't activate, and hence boost, your core during any type of exercise, but try yoga, Pilates and using a BOSU or balance ball to really enhance the muscles.

GO GO GADGET

High-tech innovations can give your training an extra dimension

Things have come a long way since the humble pedometer. As in virtually every other part of our lives, technological advances have revolutionised running. You can now plot new running routes, find buddies, track your progress and reignite your motivation at the flick of a switch and the press of a button.

> HEART RATE MONITORS

Although you can measure your heart rate without a monitor (we showed you how on page 47), it can be a faff and a tad inaccurate. A neat wrist-top gizmo will ensure you're working at the right intensity and not under- or over-training. These monitors come either with a chest strap, which sits across your torso and measures your heart beat, or without (simpler models just measure your pulse), and vary hugely in price from around £40 to £200. Popular brands include Suunto (www.suunto.com), Polar (www.polar.fi) and Garmin (www.garmin.com).

> TRACKING DEVICES

Although not always 100 per cent accurate, basic tracking devices are a great entry-level gadget to help you track your mileage and pace. They store information, which you can download on to

A MONITOR ENSURES YOU'RE WORKING AT THE RIGHT INTENSITY

your PC or Mac and this can be incredibly motivating. Most comprise a 'pod' which you place on or inside your running shoe, and a linked-up wrist monitor. The Nike+ system (www.nikerunning.nike.com) is brilliant, and check out brands such as Polar, Garmin and Suunto.

If you're not interested in precision measurements or are put off by the cost, get a sports watch so you can time your runs and interval sessions. Go for a model with memory, water-resistance and a backlight so you get the most from it.

> GPS

This is sat nav for your running! GPS systems are a step up from tracking devices and use the same principles but with greater accuracy, and you can also plot your route on them. As a result, they also tend to be more expensive. Garmin is the best-known brand, as well as Polar and Timex (www.timex.co.uk).

> APPS

There are lots of smart-phone applications for runners. Most have integrated GPS to track your routes, so there's no need for a separate gadget. Check out RunKeeper, RaceYourWorld, Runmeter, iMapMyRun and the Nike+ GPS. A good place to start is www.itunes.com/appstore.

> ONLINE ASSISTANCE

If you'd rather not invest in a gadget, you can still milk the web for its endless running resources. Use sites such as www.runfinder.co.uk to plot routes or find popular ones in your area; find running buddies via www.ffnetwork.co.uk or get advice and talk to other runners at www.runbritain.com.

Q&A

CAN I BUY HOME-GYM KIT TO HELP MY RUNNING?

Easy-to-store items such as a balance ball (also known as a Swiss ball) or BOSU (a balance disc) are great for core strength workouts. You might also consider getting a resistance band or set of free weights if you'd rather do your strengthening work at home than in the gym.

For massaging away any niggles or tension, foam rollers are a great idea. Don't forget you'll probably also need a padded mat. If you're unsure about how to use any of the kit, don't worry as most of these pieces will come with a manual packed full of information and exercises. To buy, try Argos and www.amazon.co.uk, or somewhere more fitness-focused, such as www.habdirect.co.uk or www.escapefitness.com.

THRILL OF THE RACE

Running events aren't just for elite athletes – you can get in on the act too!

Mass running events have never been more inclusive. In the Noughties, there was an explosion of emphasis-on-the-fun races and research shows more novices than ever are entering marathons. Signing up for a challenge will give you a goal to focus on and fire up your training. And when you see how far you've come, your self-esteem will soar.

MEDAL-WINNING RACE PREPARATION

Your race training should combine all the elements we've covered so far to make it as safe and enjoyable as possible.

> Have a plan – you don't have to stick to it religiously when you're a novice racer, but a structured, progressive programme (increase your mileage by no more than 10 per cent each week) is invaluable.

> To make race day as stress-free as possible, familiarise yourself with the course you're doing, or at least replicate the conditions you'll be racing in, including the time of day and terrain.

> Don't be hard on yourself. It's not unusual to feel deflated mid-training. Factor in recuperative rest days and take time out with cross-training, which will keep you fit but also give you a break from the monotony.

> If you pick up an injury, rest until you're feeling 100 per cent. A physio can advise you about other kinds of safe exercise to maintain your fitness.

> Practise with energy drinks and gels. Come race day, it's a massive error to load up on sugary sports drinks you're not used to – they can play havoc with your insides. If you're training for a long-distance event, it's crucial to identify what suits you. Read our feature on pages 106–107 for more information.

> Do your research. Know exactly where the race is, plan how you're getting to and from the event and who's coming with you.

> Make sure you wear your race outfit beforehand – it should consist of items that are comfortable and won't chafe on the day.

> Have a finish time in mind and work out your mile- or km-per-minutes rate accordingly – it will help you keep a steady pace on race day. So, if you're aiming to finish a 10k in one hour, you should be covering 1km every six minutes.

> Taper your training. In the days leading up to your race, reduce how much you're running so your body feels totally energised; normally

HAVE A GOAL FINISH TIME IN MIND AND WORK OUT YOUR DISTANCE-PER-MINUTE RATE TO HELP YOU KEEP A STEADY PACE

you'd start doing this around three days before a 5km or 10km race, up to 10 days before a half-marathon and around two to three weeks before a marathon.

FIRST-TIME ADVICE

When you're choosing a race, be realistic about your level and how far you can run efficiently without hurting yourself. Don't get fixated on 'racing' – concentrate on enjoyment and achievement. Consider these factors.

■ Give yourself plenty of time to train for the event – avoid last-minute entries for now!

■ Even if you've got your eye on something more challenging, get a taste of how it feels to run at a mass event by doing a 5k or 10k first.

■ To ease you in to racing, pick an event that's easy for you (and your support team!) to get to, preferably with a flat-ish course and a relaxed atmosphere. The bigger the event, the more likely it is to welcome novices.

■ Get friends or family involved so you can support one another on the day.

■ You can find our pick of UK races at the back of this book (pages 124–127). Remember, big events get booked up very quickly so plan ahead to avoid disappointment!

RACE DAY COMETH

From breakfast to post-event relaxation, ensure your special day is as enjoyable and pain-free as possible

THE NIGHT BEFORE

> Pack your race-day bag. Don't forget suncream, wet-wipes, sunglasses and a binbag or old top you can throw away at the race-start. Charge up your phone and iPod if you're using one.

> Lay out your clothes, making sure you choose items you've worn before. This is not the time to be trialling new things! Have your race number and safety pins ready.

> Check and double-check where and when the race start is and your travel arrangements.

> Write your estimated finish time and your split times (the time you'll reach certain points of the race) on a piece of paper and tuck it in the pocket of your shorts so you can check your pace as you run.

> Avoid alcohol and heavy meals. Sip plenty of water.

> Take a relaxing bath and get an early night.

EARLY MORNING

> Eat a familiar breakfast that you know doesn't disagree with you. Keep sipping water.

> If you have friends and family coming along, agree on a meeting point after the race.

> Get to the start as early as possible – aim for at least an hour before so you can warm up and go to the loo.

> Have a quiet moment on your own to do some deep breathing and focus on what's ahead.

AT THE START LINE

> Position yourself with people who are of a similar ability. Too far up, you may annoy elite runners, too far back and you may get impatient trying to weave through slower race-goers.

> Keep moving while you're waiting for the klaxon. Walk on the spot and keep your arms active.

> Don't get overcome by the electric atmosphere and bolt off – start slowly.

DURING THE RACE

> Continue with a steady pace and pick up confidence as you near the end.

> Don't push other runners, particularly at drink stations.

> Break the race into manageable parts – focus on the next milestone rather than the finish line.

> Slow down at drink stations and sip, rather than gulp, liquids.

STRAIGHT AFTER THE RACE

> Keep moving as you cross the finish line. Walk until your heart rate returns to normal.

> Aim to stretch every part of your body while your muscles are warm – within an hour of finishing.

> Rehydrate your body straight away and make sure you eat a snack that combines carbohydrates and protein, for example a cheese sandwich or recovery milkshake.

> Stay warm and get out of your sweaty kit as soon as possible.

> Apply ice packs to any inflamed parts of your anatomy.

THAT EVENING

> Eat an energy-rich but digestible meal such as pasta. Avoid alcohol as it may dehydrate you further.

> Get an early night to aid your muscle recovery.

IN THE DAYS FOLLOWING THE RACE

> Rest your body but don't retire to the sofa. Try some light cardio exercise, such as swimming and brisk walking, or try a relaxing yoga or Pilates class.

> Book yourself a therapeutic sports massage, but not immediately after a race when your muscles are likely to be stressed.

STRETCH YOUR BODY WHILE YOUR MUSCLES ARE STILL WARM

Q&A

HOW DO I AVOID STOMACH PROBLEMS ON THE RACE DAY?

Be it gripping pain, nausea or an urgent need for the loo, running can play havoc with your insides. Nerves can aggravate the issue if you're racing. The good news is things do normally resolve themselves although beginners tend to suffer more than experienced runners. The bad news is there's no single known cause, so working it out is down to trial and error.

Regular culprits include eating too soon before a run, dehydration, and food (or fluid) sensitivity. You can minimise the chances of an attack of the trots by allowing two to three hours between eating and running, and drinking little and often. Keep a food diary to highlight any triggers; caffeine, alcohol, dairy and fibrous foods are common culprits.

If you're racing, eat early in the morning to give your digestion plenty of time to work through whatever you've eaten, and be clear where the loos are on the course. Sip on peppermint tea to reduce any discomfort.

HALF-MARATHON PLAN

Personal trainer **Cat Dugdale**
helps you run a half-marathon

QUICK TIPS

• *Remember to warm up and stretch after each session, using our guides on pages 34–41.*

• *At least twice a week, do our strength-building exercises on pages 112–123. You can tag them on to the end of one of your run sessions. Test your fitness at the beginning and the end of the programme.*

• *This plan is designed for those with around three months' running experience to get you round a half-marathon in a moderate time. Look at our events diary on pages 124–127 for inspiration!*

WEEK	MONDAY	TUESDAY	WEDNESDAY	THURSDAY	FRIDAY	SATURDAY	SUNDAY
1	Run 2 minutes, walk 1 minute x 10	**REST**	Cross-train	Run 5km	**REST**	Run 8km	**REST**
2	Run 5km	**REST**	Cross-train	30-second sprint, 1-minute walk x 8	**REST**	Run 5–10km	**REST**
3	Run 5km	**REST**	Cross-train	30-second sprint, 1-minute walk x 8	**REST**	Run 10km time trial	**REST**
4	**REST** and massage	**REST**	Cross-train	Run 40 minutes at a comfortable pace	**REST**	Run 10km	**REST**
5	Run 5k	**REST**	Cross-train	1-minute fast-paced run, 1-minute light jog x 8	**REST** or cross-train	Run 14.5km	**REST**
6	Run 5km	**REST**	Cross-train	1-minute fast-paced run, 1-minute light jog x 8	**REST** or cross-train	Run 18km	**REST**
7	Run 5km	**REST**	Cross-train	30-second sprint, 1-minute walk x 8	**REST** or light cross-train	Run 14.5km	**REST**
8	Run 5km	**REST**	Cross-train	**REST** reward yourself	**REST** or light cross-train	Half-marathon (21km)	**CELEBRATE!**

HALF-MARATHON *PLAN*

Personal trainer **Cat Dugdale** helps you run a marathon

MARATHON PLAN

QUICK TIPS

• Remember to warm up and stretch after each session, using our guides on pages 34–41.

• At least twice a week, find the time for our strength-building exercises on pages 112–123. You can tag them on to the end of one of your run sessions. Test your fitness at the beginning, middle and towards the end of the programme.

• Only attempt this programme if you have a lot of running experience. Continue to cross-train, but, particularly during the latter stages, make sure it's something light, such as swimming, cycling on the flat, walking or gentle yoga. Do a shorter event, such as a half-marathon, before your big day.

WEEK	MONDAY	TUESDAY	WEDNESDAY	THURSDAY	FRIDAY	SATURDAY	SUNDAY
1	Run 2 minutes, walk 1 minute x 10	Cross-train	*REST*	Run 5km	*REST*	Run 8km	*REST*
2	Run 5km	30-second sprint, 1-minute walk x 8	*REST*	Cross-train	*REST*	Run 10k time trial	*REST* or light cross-train
3	Run 5km	30-second sprint, 1-minute walk x 8	*REST*	Cross-train	*REST*	Run 10km	*REST* or light cross-train
4	Run 8km	30-second sprint, 1-minute walk x 8	*REST* or cross-train	Steady 5km	*REST*	Run 14.5km	*REST* or light cross-train
5	Run 10km	1-minute fast-paced run, 1 minute light jog x 8	*REST* or cross-train	Steady 5km	*REST*	Run 18km	*REST* or light cross-train
6	Run 10km	1 minute fast-paced run, 1 minute light jog x 8	*REST* or cross-train	Steady 5km	*REST* and massage	Run 14.5km	*REST* or light cross-train
7	Run 10km	1-minute fast-paced run, 1-minute light jog x 8	*REST* or cross-train	Steady 5km	*REST*	Half-marathon (21km)	*REST* or light cross-train
8	Run 10km	30-second sprint, 1-minute walk x 8	*REST* or cross-train	Steady 5km	*REST*	Run 24km	*REST* or light cross-train
9	Run 10km	30-second sprint, 1-minute walk x 8	*REST* or cross-train	Steady 5km	*REST* and massage	Run 29km	*REST* or light cross-train
10	Run 10km	30-second sprint, 1-minute walk x 8	*REST* or cross-train	Steady 5km	*REST*	Run 35.5km	*REST* or light cross-train
11	Run 10km	Run 40 minutes at a comfy pace	*REST*	Steady 5km	*REST*	Run 10km	*REST* or light cross-train
12	Run 5km	Run for 30 minutes at a comfy pace	*REST*	Cross-train	*REST*	Marathon (42.2km)	*CELEBRATE!*

MARATHON *PLAN*

FUEL UP!

CLOTHING: Sweaty Betty, www.sweatybetty.com; American Apparel, www.americanapparel.co.uk

All the common-sense rules of healthy eating are even more important when you're a keen runner. To keep your body constantly fuelled, you need to eat well and often, and stay hydrated. Prioritise slow-burning, energy-rich complex carbohydrates, such as wholemeal pasta, rice, cereals and breads; lean muscle-building sources of protein, such as chicken, fish, tofu, legumes, and at least five daily portions of fruit and vegetables.

In this section we'll reveal everything about sound eating habits, race-day nutrition and sports supplements. We've also added some delicious recipes to tickle your taste buds.

EAT TO RUN

Fuel up sensibly and see your performance soar

EAT REGULAR MEALS

To keep your energy levels constant, establish regular eating habits – skipping meals can leave you tired, light-headed and more likely to over-eat when you do sit down for a meal. Don't leave more than four hours between meals and if you're pushed for time, choose a smart snack.

GO COMPLEX

Carbs are your muscles' key source of energy and if you don't eat enough you'll feel listless. Carbs should make up around 55 to 65 per cent of your daily calorie intake – try to choose high-fibre 'complex' versions, in other words, carbs that release energy slowly and constantly. These include oats and wholewheat pasta. When you're training for a big event such as a marathon, you may need to 'carb-load' to build up your energy reserves.

TIMING IS KEY

Top up energy and liquid levels before a run. Pre-run meals should be eaten two to three hours before to allow your stomach time to empty. Light snacks or liquid-only meals, such as a cereal bar or smoothie, are fine one to two hours before. Generally, the body has enough stored carbohydrate (glycogen) to fuel 90 minutes of continuous exercise but sports gels and sweets such as wine gums can provide a quick burst as you run.

PACK IN PROTEIN

Found in meat, poultry, pulses, dairy, fish and eggs, protein is essential for muscle repair and a vital component in the runner's diet. Aim for 1.2–1.4g per kg of your body weight, each day. If you're vegetarian or vegan, you might find this more difficult but it is possible with the addition of tofu, nuts, seeds, beans and meat substitutes such as Quorn.

RECOVERY FOOD

Within 30 minutes of finishing a run, you need to replace lost energy and boost muscle repair – try a snack bar or sports drink. Within two hours, eat a meal. Dishes rich in carbs and protein boost energy and muscle repair – try a chicken sandwich, baked potato with beans or breakfast cereal with milk. Drink plenty of fluids and avoid caffeine and alcohol, which can dehydrate you.

Q&A
I WANT TO LOSE WEIGHT BUT RUNNING IS MAKING ME HUNGRY. HELP!

To lose weight, you need to increase activity and decrease calorie intake. Use a food diary to highlight problem areas in your daily intake. Can you identify any secret calorie loaders, such as alcohol, cereal bars and sports drinks? Target these and any unhealthy cooking methods, such as frying, to streamline your habits. Make sure you're drinking plenty of water and eating fresh fruit and vegetables.

Also make sure you're doing a weekly strength session – this will help build lean muscle and therefore increase your basal metabolic rate, the rate at which your body burns energy. Finally, a note of caution; never crash diet, cut out food groups or try to lose more than one pound a week, to protect your health as well as your running progress.

BE ALCOHOL AWARE

Alcohol can dehydrate your body and is highly calorific (there are seven calories per gram and it's virtually devoid of nutrients) so stick to your recommended daily intake – for women it's two to three units of alcohol a day. Cutting back will have countless long-term health benefits.

HYDRATE YOUR BODY

Don't just think about staying hydrated during a run – get into the habit of being constantly aware of your hydration levels. Monitor the colour of your urine: if it's pale yellow, you're doing fine, but a dark yellow-orange is a sign you're not drinking enough. Find out more about hydration on pages 96–97.

FIVE ALIVE

It's important to make sure you're eating plenty of fresh fruit and vegetables – a fantastic source of fibre and a rainbow of vitamins that will ensure your immune system is fighting fit and keeping bugs at bay. One fresh juice or smoothie a day and frozen, prepared fruit and veg do count towards your daily quota.

GOOD FATS

Avoid the bad fats – saturated animal fats found in hard cheese, butter and full-fat dairy products – and go for the good varieties found in oily fish, nuts and plant oils such as olive and sunflower. These are brilliant for lowering your bad cholesterol and upping your good cholesterol, and also fantastic for keeping your joints lubricated and your skin supple.

BINGE BEWARE

Running burns lots of calories, but that doesn't mean it's a green light to eat masses. Balance is key; you need to put good-quality fuel, in the right quantities, into your body to boost your performance.

TOP FOODS FOR RUNNERS

■ **PASTA**
Eating wholewheat pasta provides slow-release energy. Combine it with lean protein for a great post-run refuel.

■ **OATS**
High in fibre and slow-release energy, porridge is a star runner's breakfast. Add fruit and seeds for extra nutrients.

■ **BANANAS**
Packed with energy and nutrients including potassium, which can help lower blood pressure.

■ **DARK, LEAFY GREENS**
Kale, cabbage, broccoli and spring greens are a great source of calcium and iron to boost your bones and energy.

■ **OILY FISH**
Fresh tuna, mackerel, sardines and salmon are a good source of protein and essential fatty acids, which are great for your heart and joints.

■ **PULSES**
They're cheap, and rich in protein, slow-release energy, fibre and nutrients including calcium. Add them to salads, soups and stews.

■ **NUTS**
Packed with essential fatty acids, heart-friendly vitamin E and protein. But nuts are calorific, so go easy on them if you're watching your weight.

■ **EGGS**
These are brimming with protein and bone-nutrient vitamin K. Choose healthy cooking methods, such as poaching or scrambling.

THE RULES OF HYDRATION

What you drink is just as important as what you eat if you want to run your best

Water makes up around 60 per cent of your total weight and plays a vital role in each and every bodily process. It's so vital in fact that experts say if you are just two per cent dehydrated, your performance could drop by a whopping 10 per cent.

An average person, in normal weather conditions, needs to drink around two litres of water a day. But when you're exercising regularly, sweating one to two litres an hour, your needs are greatly increased. Fail to consume enough and you risk developing headaches, fatigue and even heat exhaustion and impaired heart function.

DRINKING GUIDE

➤ The best way to check your level of hydration is to look at your urine, which should be the colour of pale straw or crisp white wine. If it's a dark yellow-orange, you're not drinking enough.

➤ In general, it's best to drink little and often throughout the day, rather than gulping down fluids intermittently. Keep a water bottle with you and a glass on your desk.

➤ In the hour before a run, drink up to half a litre of water, slowly and steadily. During your run, aim for 250ml every 15 minutes, but be guided by your thirst.

➤ The best test of how much you need to drink is to weigh yourself before and after a run – the amount of weight you lose is the amount you need to replace. But that's not practical for most of us, so listen to your body and continue to pace your fluid intake after you've finished. Aim for at least 500ml, sipped slowly.

➤ During tough training sessions, try sipping sports drinks containing electrolytes to replace energy and the salts you've lost through sweating. You can make your own by diluting fruit squash and adding a pinch of salt.

Q&A

CAN I RUN OFF A HANGOVER?

Absolutely not. Your body is designed to deal with alcohol at a set rate of about a unit an hour and you can't accelerate this. In general, high alcohol intake and exercise don't mix; alcohol is a diuretic so it dehydrates your body, numbs your reaction times and disturbs sleep, which is essential for muscle renewal. Its immediate effect is to kick the liver – a big energy guzzler – into action. This diverts energy away from your muscles and your heart, which then have to rely on your anaerobic system, which in turn, increases your risk of pain and cramps. Since the heart is sensitised, pushing it could lead to arrhythmia or palpitations. And it goes without saying that if you've got a thumping headache, dull reflexes and an overwhelming sense of nausea, there's no way you're going to be putting in maximum effort.

If you have a hangover, drink lots of water, take a painkiller, eat something nutritious and take some low-intensity exercise, such as a brisk walk.

SIP SPORTS DRINKS TO REPLACE ENERGY AND SALTS LOST IN SWEAT

TOO MUCH OF A GOOD THING?

Although dehydration is more common than over-hydration, long-distance runners should be aware of the danger of excessive water consumption. Hyponatraemia means low concentration of sodium in the blood, and can be avoided with our constant and steady approach to drinking. If you're doing a long run or event, don't guzzle too much fluid on your way round, and try a sports drink to replace lost salts. Hyponatraemia symptoms include vomiting, dizziness and confusion.

RUNNING MEALS

MEALS FOR RUNNERS

Fuel up and recover with these tempting high-energy recipes

POWER PORRIDGE

Stay energised all day with this super-nutritious breakfast.
SERVES 1

■ Add one mug of oats, two mugs of water, half an organic apple, chopped, one heaped tablespoon of raisins and one teaspoon of cinnamon to a pan. Bring to the boil, then turn down the heat and stir regularly for four to five minutes.

■ Stir in ¼ to ½ mug of milk and bring back to almost boiling. Add the other half of the apple, stir and put into a bowl.

■ Drizzle with one tablespoon of blackstrap molasses and sprinkle with one tablespoon of pumpkin seeds.

SPAGHETTI BOLOGNESE

Try this vegetarian twist on the famous pasta dish.
SERVES 6

■ Put a dash of sunflower oil in a pan and brown one finely chopped red onion, stirring regularly.

■ Add a finely diced carrot, ½ red, ½ yellow and ½ green pepper, all finely chopped, and 1 finely diced courgette. Cook gently for 10 mins.

■ Add 2–4 cloves crushed garlic, 1 teaspoon dried basil, 2 teaspoons dried oregano, a pinch of salt and pepper. Stir for a minute then add a glass of dry wine, 1 x 400g tin Puy lentils and 2 x 400g tin tomatoes.

■ Bring to a simmer, cover and cook for 15 minutes, stirring occasionally and adding a little water if needed.

■ Cook the spaghetti and drain.

■ Mix the sauce into the cooked spaghetti. Top with chopped fresh parsley and basil and serve.

CHILLI

Feed a crowd with this low-fat , veggie spin on the Mexican dish.
SERVES 10

■ Place a large pan on a medium heat, add a dash of sunflower oil and 2 chopped onions and brown for 10 minutes, stirring regularly.

■ Chop 3 mixed peppers, 1 large carrot, 1 courgette, 1 aubergine, 1 apple and set aside.

■ Drain and rinse 1 x 400g can Puy lentils, 1 x 400g can kidney beans and 1 x 400g can cannelini beans. Mix 2 teaspoons oregano, 2 teaspoons cumin, 1 teaspoon paprika, 1 teaspoon chilli and 1 teaspoon salt in a small bowl.

■ Add the fresh vegetables and the apple to the pan and stir regularly for another 10 minutes.

■ Add 2 x 400g tins of chopped tomatoes, 350ml boiling water and the herb and spice mixture to the pan, return to a gentle boil. Add the beans and lentils, reduce the heat, cover with a lid and simmer gently for 25 minutes. Season to taste.

ULTIMATE BREAKFAST SMOOTHIE

This smoothie is crammed with nutrients and is high in fibre and protein, so it's filling too. Packed with vitamin C, berries are a quick and easy ingredient for smoothies, especially in the morning when you don't have time to peel and chop fruit. Frozen berries are extra convenient. SERVES 1

■ Add 80g frozen raspberries, 80g frozen blueberries, 200ml oat milk, two heaped tablespoons live natural yoghurt, 100g silken tofu and one tablespoon runny honey to a jug and blend until smooth.

■ To save time, pop everything into a jug the night before, leave in the fridge then just blend in the morning.

BUTTERNUT AND ALLIUM SOUP

Boost your immune system with this antioxidant-rich soup.
SERVES 4

■ Add a dash of sunflower oil, three chopped onions, a peeled, deseeded and chopped butternut squash and two sliced leeks to the pan and stir for five minutes.

■ Add four to six cloves of crushed garlic, one heaped teaspoon of turmeric, one teaspoon of chilli flakes and 3cm of fresh ginger, peeled and grated. Stir, then add one litre of chicken stock. Bring to the boil, stir, then cover and simmer for 15 minutes.

■ Blend the soup and season to taste. Pour into bowls and sprinkle with freshly ground black pepper and fresh chives.

APPLE AND BLACKBERRY CRUMBLE

A guilt-free pudding packed with superfoods.
SERVES 6

■ Put 4 slices crumbled wholemeal bread, 50g rolled oats and 50g ground almonds in a bowl and mix well.

■ Roughly chop 4 unpeeled, cored Cox apples into chunks and put in an ovenproof dish.

■ Sprinkle a 200g punnet of blackberries over the apples then add half a cup of apple juice.

■ Sprinkle the crumble mixture evenly over the fruit, then drizzle with 2 tablespoons runny honey.

■ Bake in a pre-heated oven at 200°C/gas mark 6 for 15–20 minutes until golden brown.

■ Serve immediately with a little natural yoghurt or crème fraîche.

WILTED WATERCRESS WITH GOAT'S CHEESE ON GARLIC TOAST

This healthy snack is a great source of iron, calcium and antioxidant vitamins and is delicious too.
SERVES 2

▪ Lightly brown 2 teaspoons of pine nuts in a dry frying pan.

▪ Toast four slices ciabatta, then rub them with a peeled clove of garlic and put them onto a plate.

▪ Add a little olive oil to a large hot pan and toss in 1 bag of watercress until it starts to wilt.

▪ Heap the watercress onto the bread and sprinkle with crumbled goat's cheese and pine nuts. Drizzle with olive oil and balsamic vinegar, plus freshly ground black pepper, and serve.

NEW POTATOES AND ASPARAGUS

Not just top running fuel, potatoes are also full of vitamins B and C, minerals and fibre.

SERVES 4–6

■ Trim the ends off a bunch of asparagus and cut into 3cm pieces, reserving the tips.

■ Take 500g new potatoes, cut the larger ones in half, leave the rest whole. Boil for 15 minutes, then add the asparagus stems, cover and cook for five minutes.

■ Add the asparagus tips, cook for a few more minutes, drain and season with salt and pepper, chopped parsley and spring onion.

■ Toss with a little extra virgin olive oil and serve hot or cold.

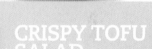

CRISPY TOFU SALAD

Tofu is a great source of low-fat protein and calcium.

SERVES 2 (AS A MAIN COURSE)

■ Cut a block of firm tofu into thin slices and pat dry.

■ Slice 4 spring onions and mix with 2cm freshly grated ginger root, ½ sliced red chilli, 1 crushed clove garlic and 2 teaspoons toasted sesame oil.

■ Arrange a 200g bag of mixed salad leaves on two plates. Add a little sunflower oil to a pan and cook the tofu until crisp on both sides. Remove from the pan and reserve. Add the spring onion mix and cook for a few minutes, stirring. Add the tofu, stir then add 2 teaspoons soy sauce, 2 teaspoons honey and juice of ½ a lime. Spoon onto the leaves and serve.

EVENT EATING

How to fuel your body for a race

Now you know the bedrock principles of healthy eating, here's how to fine-tune your diet in order to prepare properly for your next running event.

DURING THE PRECEDING WEEKS...

> Practise using energy drinks and gels so you know what your stomach can tolerate and what works for you. And learn how to use them 'on the run'. Don't trial anything on race day! Also test race-day breakfasts – good choices include porridge, scrambled egg on wholemeal bread or muesli with banana and milk or yoghurt.
> Remember to keep drinking little and often and to monitor the colour of your urine.
> Up your calorie intake – when you're increasing your mileage, you need to up the amount you're eating too. Women are recommended to take in 1,940 calories per day but your age, weight, height, body composition and activity levels affect this.
> Make sure you're eating a wide range of fresh fruit and vegetables – they're packed with antioxidants to support your immune system and keep bugs at bay.
> Get into the habit of healthy snacking (see pages 94–95 for ideas) – an easy way to add calories and keep your energy levels constant.

THE WEEK BEFORE...

> By now you should have decided on your race-day foods, from breakfast to energy drinks.
> Eat and drink little and often so your energy stays constant and you don't feel bloated.
> Increase the amount of carbs you're eating ('carb loading') – the ideal is to get 60–70 per cent of your calories from carbs. Make sure you choose slow-energy-release foods (low-glycaemic), such as wholegrains, to promote glycogen storage.

EAT AND DRINK LITTLE AND OFTEN SO YOUR ENERGY IS CONSTANT

THE DAY BEFORE...

> Stick with what you know – this isn't the time to be getting adventurous with your foods. Minimise fibrous foods that will send your digestion awry.
> Avoid alcohol so you feel at your best and hydrated tomorrow!
> Don't overindulge – eat little and often. Go for a high-carb, low-fat and moderate-protein balance.

THE MORNING BEFORE...

> To allow time to process your breakfast, eat early. Avoid caffeine if it irritates your bowel.
> Aim to drink around 400 to 600ml of water, a sports drink or diluted fruit juice about two hours before the race.

DURING THE RACE...

> Drink every 20 minutes – make the most of drink stations.
> Pace your energy extras, such as gels – they'll provide energy for around 30 to 45 minutes of exercise.

AFTER THE RACE...

> Aim to drink around 500ml slowly within 30 minutes of finishing.
> If your appetite is suppressed, ease yourself into eating with a high-carb snack within the first 30 minutes.
> Within two hours, eat a light meal comprising protein and refuelling carbs – try a tuna or cheese sandwich for instance. Keep snacking throughout the day and choose easy-to-digest foods, such as pasta or a baked potato for your dinner.
> Bypass the alcohol, junk food and caffeine.

Q&A

WHAT IS 'THE WALL'?

This phrase refers to the point at which your body's glycogen stores run out and blood sugar levels trough, leaving you weak, dizzy and nauseous. It's usually something only full-marathoners will experience (apparently around four out of 10) as your body can store enough to carry you through shorter distances.

The key to avoiding 'the wall' is a sound pre-race eating habit and regular carb consumption during the race (30 to 60g for every hour). If you want to find out more, a US academic has worked out a formula to help runners calculate how much carbohydrate you should eat to stop your fuel reserves running out. See endurancecalculator.com.

ENERGY
EXTRAS

Sports-specific food
and drink for runners

Although a healthy diet is vital to your fitness and running performance, active bodies with high-energy needs can sometimes benefit from a few extras. However, you should approach sports drinks and snacks with caution as they tend to be sugary and, as a result, calorific and bad for your teeth. Use them in moderation to supplement, rather than replace, a balanced diet and try out a few options to see what best suits your taste buds and your stomach.

You'll regularly come across terms such as 'isotonic' – which means the drink has the same concentration as your body's natural fluids and therefore is more readily absorbed than water; and 'electrolytes', which are salts to replace what's lost through sweating.

ENERGY GELS

These are an acquired taste, but are convenient to use when you're on the move. Some runners love them, some hate them. They normally come in foil sachets so you can squirt the gel into your mouth. The consistency's like runny jam and the gels come in flavours such as blackcurrant and strawberry. You must drink fluid with them – around 200ml per sachet – so you can absorb them. Popular brands include Science in Sport (SiS; www.scienceinsport.com), Maxim (www.maxim.nl) and Lucozade (www.lucozadeshop.com).

ENERGY BARS

Eat these pre- or post-run. They tend to be carb-rich, but you'll also encounter nutrition, sports or recovery bars, which contain protein. Energy bars can be cloying and sweet but are very convenient, especially if you're too rushed to prepare your own snack. They also come in a myriad of flavours, so there's bound to be one to suit you. Again, remember to take on enough water when you're having a bar. Big brands include High5 (www.highfive.co.uk), Maximuscle (www.maximuscle.com) and SiS (www.scienceinsport.com).

SPORTS DRINKS

These rehydrate you and fuel your muscles. Fluid replacement drinks are ideal if you're only sweating lightly and just need hydration as they contain less than four per cent carbs. Isotonic drinks contain four to eight per cent carbs and sodium to replace salts lost in sweat – use during or after intense exercise.

OTHER OPTIONS…

MEAL-REPLACEMENT SHAKES Versions such as For Goodness Shakes (www.forgoodnessshakes.com) contain protein and are best consumed after exercise.

SPORTS SWEETS OR LOZENGES Sport Beans (www.sportbeans.co.uk) and similar are an ultra-convenient energy hit during your runs.

SUPPLEMENTS A balanced diet should provide all the nutrients you need, but supplements are a simple and convenient way to get the boost you want; brands include Wellwoman (www.vitabiotics.com), Reflex (www.reflex-nutrition.com), Solgar (www.solgar.co.uk), AthletEQ (www.athleteq.co.uk) and Bio-Synergy (www.bio-synergy.co.uk).

NATURAL SPORTS FOODS AND DRINK There's a growing range of more natural products, such as coconut water (Vita Coco; www.vitacoco.com) and wholefood energy bars, such as Mule (www.mulebar.com). These are great if you want to bypass the additives.

Q&A
CAN I RUN WHEN I'M PREGNANT?

It really depends on your activity levels before your pregnancy. Medical opinion is agreed that exercise is safe – even essential – during a healthy pregnancy. If you have running experience, it should be fine to continue light, steady runs during your first trimester and second trimester. In your third trimester, it's advisable to swap to something low-impact, such as swimming or gentle pregnancy-specific yoga classes. You shouldn't start running for the first time or enter an event at any stage of pregnancy. Always seek the advice of your midwife.

GYM WORK

Running will strengthen your muscles, but you need to add a sophisticated resistance workout to maximise your performance. Gym work will improve your overall body composition, prevent imbalances – and crucially, protect you from injury. Studies also show building powerful muscles strengthens your bones, tweaks your posture and improves your running.

RESISTANCE TRAINING
FOR RUNNERS

How gym work can boost your running performance

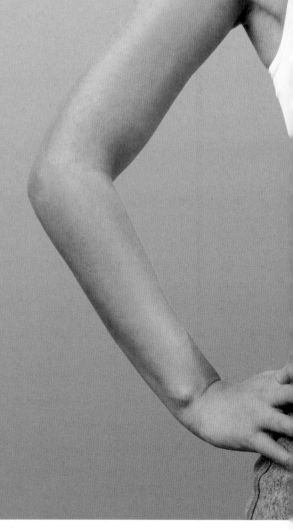

Sometimes it can be hard to find the time for other forms of exercise, but even if you're feeling squeezed, you should try to prioritise run-specific strength sessions in the gym or at home. Here's why.

> Stronger connective tissues (ligaments and tendons).
> Increased muscle mass and hence, better body composition.
> Improved co-ordination, balance and core strength.
> Balanced, robust and less injury-prone muscles.
> Improved running economy (the amount of energy expended when you run).
> Stronger bones – if the tissues are stronger, your bone density is improved.
> Renewed enthusiasm for running! Strength training is a respite for your body and mind.

WHAT TO DO

We've included a body maintenance programme (pages 112–123), which is perfect for seasoned runners. It focuses on strengthening the stabilising muscles that are needed to keep your pelvis level while running and to prevent your legs rolling in. It also hones the thigh and bottom muscles to give you a more powerful stride and help you run further. We've added exercises using a couple of pieces of equipment including a Swiss ball and a medicine ball that will test your core strength.

This programme is not meant to be a full-body strength workout. If you do decide to do a full resistance session each week, make sure you have a rest day the following day.

Q&A

CAN I DO STRETCHES OR STRENGTH EXERCISES DURING MY RUN OUTDOORS?

Of course! As well as helping to ease out your muscles, stopping to do a few stretches or exercises can break up the monotony of a run. Use the natural environment around you – trees, benches, kerbs and steps – as props. Try these stretches.

> Kerb calf stretch: with one foot fully on the kerb, bend at the hips and knee and drop the heel of your other foot off the edge. Hold for 20 seconds, then swap legs.

> Hamstring stretch: stand behind a bench or seat, resting one heel on the back of the bench. Lift from the hips and push your chest forward over your leg. Hold for 20 seconds; swap legs.

You can do technique drills outdoors and some of the resistance exercises detailed overleaf, too. Try a set of step-ups on a stable and secure bench, driving your knee up to your chest as you do so, or use a bench as a prop for press-ups or triceps dips.

THE RUNNER'S WORKOUT

These exercises will build strength and stability to improve your running performance

TIP

Try to do this routine two to three times a week. Remember to keep good posture throughout, move slowly and don't rush, jerk or bounce any of the poses.

1 THE CLAM

ACTIVATES THE GLUTEAL MUSCLES, TO HELP STABILISE THE HIPS

■ Lie on your side, with your head resting on your outstretched arm and a resistance band around your lower thighs. Your spine should be in neutral, your legs together and bent, and your heels in line with your bottom. Engage your core muscles (a).

■ Open the top knee as far as you can without moving your spine or rolling back (b). Hold for six to 10 seconds, then – with control – return your top leg back down to the starting position.

■ Repeat 10 times, then repeat on the other side to complete one set. Perform three sets.

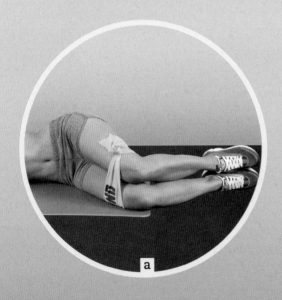

2 SCOOTER

WORKS YOUR CORE MUSCLES, GLUTEALS AND STRENGTHENS THE QUADRICEPS. ALSO IMPROVES YOUR BALANCE WHICH CAN INCREASE YOUR STRIDE LENGTH

■ Engaging your core, stand on your right leg and bend your right knee slightly (a).

■ Keeping your pelvis level and your deep abdominals working, lean forward to balance your weight over the standing leg.

■ Extend your left leg out behind you, straightening the leg, making sure you don't arch your back (b). Then bring your left leg up in front of you, again without rounding your spine or lifting your hip.

■ Repeat 15 times, then repeat on the other side to complete one set. Perform three sets.

a

b

3 GLUTEAL SWISS BALL ROLL

GREAT FOR THE GLUTEALS AND INCREASING HIP STABILITY

■ Place the ball between you and the wall. With your right side to the wall, stand on your left leg and rest your bent right leg against the ball, keeping the ball about a foot off the floor (a).

■ Gently contract your buttock muscles to stabilise you, and push into the wall with your right knee without moving the pelvis or spine. Using your knee, slowly roll the ball a few inches forward then back along the wall (b).

■ Roll the ball for 30 seconds on each leg. Repeat three times.

4 SINGLE LEG SQUAT

IMPROVES BALANCE AND PELVIC STABILITY AND STRENGTHENS THE GLUTEALS AND QUADRICEPS

■ Stand on your right leg with your abs engaged and your back straight. Bend your left leg, lifting the heel behind you and keeping both knees in line. Now, bend your right leg as far as you can, ensuring the knee moves directly over the fourth toe. Visualise your leg turning out from the hip.

■ Allow your torso to hinge forward from the hips, but don't let the pelvis 'dip' to the side (pictured). Pause, straighten and repeat. Do two sets of 15 reps on each leg.

5 TOWEL GRAB

THIS STRENGTHENS THE MUSCLES IN YOUR FEET AND CALVES WHICH CAN HELP PREVENT INJURIES

■ Remove your shoes and stand with feet hip-distance apart on a folded towel (a). Activating your toes and arches, try and pull the towel back with your feet (b).
■ Hold for five seconds and release. Do three sets of 15 reps.

a

b

6 ANKLE FLEXION/TOE RAISE

PARTICULARLY GOOD FOR OVER-PRONATORS, THIS STRENGTHENS YOUR SHINS, WHICH CAN HELP PREVENT SHIN SPLINTS. IT ALSO BOOSTS LOWER-BODY STRENGTH AND STABILITY

■ Stand with your back against the wall and flex your feet up towards your body (a). Let them drop slightly, using your shin muscles (tibialis anterior) to stop them dropping completely down to the floor (b).

■ Repeat 10 times, then flex them again and pulse for 20 reps. Do a total of three sets.

a

b

7 DEAD BUG

THIS WORKS THE DEEP CORE MUSCLES THAT HELP STABILISE AND PROTECT YOUR LOWER BACK

■ Lie on your back on a mat, with your knees up and bent at 90° and arms straight up in the air above your shoulders (a). Slowly lower your right arm behind your head and straighten your left leg towards the floor while keeping your lower back on the mat (b). Return to the starting position, then lower the left arm and right leg towards the floor.

■ Repeat three sets of 10 reps on each side.

8 BRIDGE
THIS HELPS PREVENT YOU 'SITTING' ON THE PELVIS WHEN YOU'RE RUNNING

■ Lie on your back with your knees bent and your heels close to your bottom, with arms folded across your chest.

■ Slowly curl your spine up off the floor, starting at the tailbone, until your body forms a straight line from shoulders to knees (pictured). Hold for five seconds (building up to 10 seconds), keeping your knees together. Lower your spine in reverse, vertebra by vertebra until your tailbone reaches the mat. Repeat 10 times to complete one set; perform three sets.

GYM WORK BRIDGE

9 RESISTANCE LUNGE

IMPROVES THIGH AND GLUTEAL STRENGTH AND OPENS UP YOUR HIPS

■ Start with your feet roughly hip distance apart. Place a resistance band under your right foot and hold with both hands.

■ Keeping hold of the band, take a big step back with your left leg onto the ball of your foot. Keep your gaze forward and your torso upright (a).

■ Smoothly bend both knees until your right thigh is parallel to the floor, keeping your right knee over your right foot (b). Slowly return to the start position with control.

■ Aim for two sets of 10 reps on each side.

10 BALL ROLL-IN
WORKS THE HAMSTRINGS, BOTTOM AND LOWER BACK

■ Lie on your back with your heels on a Swiss ball, legs straight and arms by your sides. Raise your hips so your body forms a straight line from head to heels (a).

■ Bending your knees, roll the ball in towards your bottom while keeping your hips lifted (b). Pause, then slowly extend your legs again. To progress, do the same exercise with your arms folded across your chest to challenge your stability.

■ Repeat 10 times to complete one set; perform three sets.

a

b

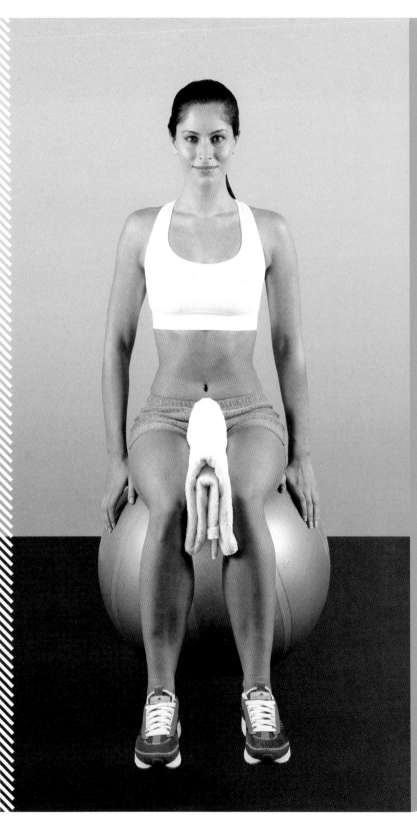

11 CUSHION SQUEEZE

REDUCES KNEE INJURY RISK, IMPROVES STRENGTH IN INNER THIGHS AND GLUTEALS

■ Sit upright on a chair or Swiss ball with a folded towel or cushion between your knees and your feet parallel. Engage your abs and look straight ahead, hands on hips or resting lightly on the ball.

■ Squeeze the towel/cushion for 10 seconds, contracting your gluteals at the same time. Gradually release, but don't let the cushion drop. Repeat 10 times to complete one set; perform two sets.

12 KNEE DRIVE

GREAT FOR BUILDING UP STRENGTH IN YOUR GLUTEALS AND HAMSTRINGS

■ Place your right foot flat on a sturdy step or stair, keeping your left foot on the floor in a semi-lunge position (a).

■ Using your arms to drive you, bring your left knee up towards your chest so it reaches a 90° angle (b). Keep your right foot stable throughout. Return to the starting position and repeat 15 times on each leg to complete one set. Perform two sets.

EVENTS
DIARY

There's a race out there to suit
everyone, so sign up today!

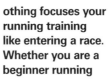

Nothing focuses your running training like entering a race. Whether you are a beginner running your first 5k, or a more experienced runner looking forward to the challenge of your first marathon, there's definitely a race for you! Here is our pick of UK events; to find alternative races near you, visit www.runningdiary.co.uk and www.runbritain.com.

UNDER 10K

RACE FOR LIFE
The largest women-only fundraising event in the UK comprises more than 200 runs taking place from May to July. In addition to the regular 5k runs, some locations offer a 10k route; *www.raceforlife.org.*

PARKRUN
Free, weekly and open to everyone, parkrun organises 5km timed runs around the UK; *parkrun.com.*

BUPA GREAT WINTER RUN
Kick start your new year with this 5k road run in January in the gorgeous surroundings of Holyrood Park in Edinburgh. For all abilities; *www.greatrun.org.*

ADIDAS WOMEN'S 5K CHALLENGE
A welcoming September run for women of all ages and abilities in Hyde Park, London; *www.womenschallenge.co.uk.*

BHF SANTA JOGS
Get into the Christmas spirit with the British Heart Foundation's festive fancy dress dashes, ranging from 2 to 5k, around the UK in late November and December; *www.bhf.org.uk*

10K AND OVER

THE MIGHTY DEERSTALKER
Not the average event! Run 10k at night or 5k before the daylight fades, around the grounds of historic Traquair House in Peeblesshire, Scotland in March. Lycra optional – most runners tackle the off-road route wearing tweed and a hat; *www.themightydeerstalker.com.*

RACE FOR LIFE IS THE LARGEST WOMEN-ONLY UK FUNDRAISING RUN

CANCER RESEARCH 10K
More than 20 events, all over the country in early autumn – great for 10k novices. Visit *www. cancerresearchuk.org/10k.*

BUPA GREAT SOUTH RUN
A fast, flat course through Southsea and Portsmouth. Europe's leading 10-mile road race takes place in October; *www.greatrun.org.*

BUPA LONDON 10,000
A scenic 10k May jaunt starting close to Buckingham Palace, via iconic landmarks including Nelson's Column and the London Eye; *www.london10000.co.uk.*

LEEDS 10K
Founded by the inspirational Jane Tomlinson, this June race

suits any level and ability. There are further 10k races in Hull and York if you're Yorkshire based; *www.runforall.com.*

THE NEW FOREST 10
A 10-mile road and forest track event through this gorgeous National Park in July; nf10.co.uk/.

SALOMON FOREST TRAILS
If you want to try off-road, this series of mid-week 10k events is a great chance to sample the wonders of trail running. www.salomontrails.com/10k-forest-trails.php

GREAT SCOTTISH RUN
Enter either a 10k or half marathon around Glasgow. Takes place every September, attracting over 20,000 runners; *www.runglasgow.org.*

HALF-MARATHONS
ROYAL PARKS HALF-MARATHON
This 13.1-mile October event is a leafy jaunt through central London's Royal Parks including Kensington Gardens; *www.royalparkshalf.com.*

BUPA GREAT NORTH RUN
The biggest half-marathon in the UK, maybe the world! The September run from Newcastle to South Shields attracts an awe-inspiring 50,000 runners; *www.greatrun.org*

THE SOUTH COAST HALF-MARATHON
Drink in scenic seafront views on this race around the town of Seaford in East Sussex. Takes place in August, with additional 5k and 10k events; *www.southcoastrun.co.uk.*

BRISTOL HALF-MARATHON
Usually run in September, the course starts and finishes in Bristol's historic harbour side, passing twice under the famous Clifton Suspension Bridge; *www.bristolhalfmarathon.com.*

ADIDAS HALF-MARATHON AT SILVERSTONE
Discover Silverstone, the home of British Grand Prix, on two feet rather than four wheels! Takes place in March; *www.adidashalfmarathon.co.uk.*

RUN TO THE BEAT
The course starts and finishes at London's O2 Arena (formerly the Millennium Dome) and weaves around historic Greenwich, with plenty of music along the way. Usually late September, early October; *www.runtothebeat.co.uk.*

CARDIFF HALF-MARATHON
A flat, fast and incredibly scenic October route, that begins and finishes in Cardiff Bay; *www.cardiffhalfmarathon.co.uk*

MULL OF KINTYRE HALF-MARATHON
Can't be beaten for scenic views! A multi-terrain race, including a stretch of beach – there's a 10k option, too. Takes place in May; *www.mokrun.com.*

MARATHONS
VIRGIN LONDON MARATHON
The most famous of them all. Every April, it welcomes more than 30,000 elite and novice runners on a varied route from Greenwich to the Mall; *www.virginlondonmarathon.com*

LOCH NESS MARATHON
The Loch Ness Marathon and Festival of Running in October includes a 26.2-mile course from Fort Augustus past Loch Ness into Inverness but also 5k and 10k races for those wanting shorter events; *www.lochnessmarathon.com*

SNOWDONIA MARATHON
Only the brave need apply! A challenging October run in the scenic environs of Snowdonia; *www.snowdoniamarathon.co.uk.*

BRIGHTON MARATHON
One of the newest marathons on the circuit, it takes place in April. The race starts in Preston Park and takes in Brighton Pavilion and stunning stretches of coastal road; *www.brightonmarathon.co.uk.*

EDINBURGH MARATHON FESTIVAL
The Edinburgh Marathon Festival over two days in May offers a race for all levels: a full marathon, half marathon, 10k, 5k and junior race; *www.edinburgh-marathon.com.*

BRATHAY WINDERMERE MARATHON, CUMBRIA
A gorgeous circuit of Windermere, England's largest lake, which attracts around 10,000 runners every May; *www.brathaywindermeremarathon.org.uk.*

BEACHY HEAD MARATHON
One of the biggest off-road marathons in the UK and a scenic and challenging route through the South Downs National Park; *www.visiteastbourne.com/events.*

THE BUPA GREAT SOUTH
RUN IS EUROPE'S TOP
10-MILE ROAD RACE

*PARTICIPANTS ENJOYING THE
BUPA GREAT SOUTH RUN 2010*

TRACK YOUR PROGRESS

Use a running diary to refine your training and motor your motivation

You can buy or download a training log with relative ease, but if you want to make your own, use this template as a guide.

To make your diary into a real keepsake, buy a special notebook or set up a dedicated spreadsheet. There are no rules about what information to include – you might prefer minimal entries because it makes your log easier to keep up. However, using pictures and adding extra details such as the weather conditions and your mood give it extra resonance. Make it personal to you!

Every week, sit down to plan runs for the seven days ahead and flick back over the preceding months. Use it to identify any problems in your training and your strengths, to rally your confidence when you're feeling down, and above all, remind yourself of just how far you've come!

2011 Monday 27 June

TIME OF DAY: Morning, before work

WEATHER: Raining and cold!

ROUTE (INCLUDING TERRAIN TYPE): Round park, hilly

DISTANCE: 5K

SESSION TYPE: Steady run

TIME: 31 mins

HEART RATE (RESTING/AVERAGE/MAXIMUM OR RECOVERY): 170 maximum – recovered well

HOW IT FELT: Tough start but got easier!

POSITIVES: Faster than last week by 1 minute

NEGATIVES: Wet and soggy trainers

NOTES: (INCLUDING WHO YOU RAN WITH AND WHAT YOU ATE AND DRANK BEFORE AND AFTER)

On my own, had a banana before run and porridge with berries for breakfast afterwards.

SIGN OFF

WITH THANKS TO...

personal trainer Cat Dugdale for creating the running plans in this book. Cat is the body and the brains behind SUPERchick, a female-focused fitness training brand (www.iamsuper chick.com). A former professional dancer, she has 10 years' experience in the fitness industry. Cat lives in London and fits in a run most days of the week.

This has been a book of firsts. Your first 15 minutes of non-stop running, your first pair of running trainers and your first race. You're hopefully feeling fitter, fired up and enjoying the many benefits running offers. So where next, you're asking? The possibilities are endless because, as you may have gathered from our enthusiasm, running is the most versatile and adaptable activity. Sign up for a longer race, try a triathlon or duathlon, join a local running club, find a running buddy, pass the running bug onto friends and family or sample the joys of trail and fell running. Stay healthy, injury-free and above all...

Keep running!